IN LEAGUE WITH THE FUTURE

Walter R. Wietzke

IN LEAGUE WITH THE FUTURE

The People of God in Ministry

AUGSBURG Publishing House • Minneapolis

CONTENTS

INTRODUCTION

Theology and preaching are futile exercises if they are not grounded in the business of living in a far from perfect world. Their task is indeed a daunting one. It is to do some sort of justice to the dimension of the ultimate in the midst of human finitude, to speak meaningfully of the final mysteries in what remains of this tormented century. This is precisely what Dr. Walter Wietzke's book does. Written by a dedicated churchman, a fine theologian. and according to his own peers, an outstanding preacher, it speaks appositely to our condition.

The author is neither an iconoclast nor a starry-eyed optimist. An experienced pastor, he knows, more than most, that it is folly to invest institutional religion with any pretense of infallibility. His critics—who hasn't got them?—cannot possibly accuse him of docetism. His faith, far from being disembodied and dehumanized, is tethered to the solid earth. The language he uses is arrestingly contemporary.

Dr. Wietzke grapples with certain areas of Christian communication which are of supreme importance if Christians are to witness effectively in their time. No doubt there are other areas of concern which he could have discussed profitably, but like life itself, the writing of a book demands a sense of priorities. In view of the challenge which the church faces, I am sure he has made the proper selection.

One area is the ecumenical scandal. We all know that there is a great deal of pussyfooting in so called inter-church dialogues. Denominations, while acknowledging the universal nature of the church—the body of Christ—have nevertheless succumbed to structural fundamentalism. In claiming that certain ecclesiastical structures belong to the *esse* of the church, they are guilty of idolatry, the absolutising of that which is merely relative. Dr. Wietzke, a Lutheran, proud of his tradition, has no mercy on any form of stultifying provincialism. He speaks for universal man.

Another area he deals with is that of theology. On no account will he allow a pastor or a preacher to regard theology as an extra tagged on to his training. To him the discipline of theology is basic to a healthy ministry. Without critical reflection, we are not likely to engage intelligently with a secular culture. While Dr. Wietzke believes theology, properly understood, is always church oriented, he makes a powerful plea for the maximum intellectual freedom which implies the asking of awkward questions.

Finally, he argues that faith, worship and theology must be related to meaningful action in society. At this point in his thinking, he shows an extraordinary kinship with Professor John Macmurray, who in all his works, stresses the indissoluble unity of knowledge and action. In the passage on the relation of conscience and courage, Dr. Wietzke is also one with Arthur Koestler. This indeed is the main thrust of *Darkness at Noon*, perhaps the greatest political novel of the twentieth century.

This book is at one and the same time helpful and disturbing. It combines perceptive analysis of the state of the church with prophetic anticipation of the shape of things to come. It should be made required reading in all theological faculties and seminaries, irrespective of the particular tradition.

Murdo Ewen Macdonald
University of Glasgow
Glasgow, Scotland

PREFACE

On January 3, 1882, Henrik Ibsen wrote a letter to Georg Brandes in which he said, "I hold that man is in the right who is most closely in league with the future." His sentiment is seminal for the following statement on ministry. While I make some claim regarding originality of content, I am totally obligated to Ibsen regarding the form of title.

Analogically "I hold that church to be in the right which is most closely in league with the future," that is, the future which God has ordained, which is eschatologically given in the Scriptures, and to which he calls the congregations and denominations of this day.

Consciousness of that future is a burgeoning phenomenon in Lutheranism. We increasingly echo the sentiment "I (find) that my religious reflection is tending to concentrate not on religion as it has been or is now, but upon its future—upon what it can be and will be." (John Macmurray, *Search for Reality in Religion*, pp. 1-2.)

This discourse is dedicated to God's future and to all who strive to make that essential in dealing with our common human present, especially my wife Gloria, our sons and daughters, Sandra, Robert, Walter, Karol and Mark, and my colleague, the Reverend Wayne C. Stumme.

W.R.W.

1 TOWARD A DEFINITION OF MINISTRY

A public affirmation of trust is always a great boost for church people. Out of the Princeton Religion Resource Center and the American Institute of Public Opinion comes substantial evidence that Christians generally, and Christian clergy particularly, have more credibility than they usually dream about. Peruse, therefore, these supportive examples published by colleagues from the Fourth Estate:

Honesty and Ethical Standards

Question: "How would you rate the honesty and ethical standards of people in these different fields—very high, high, average, low or very low?"

	Very High	High	Average	Low	Very Low	No Opinion
Clergymen	21%	40%	30%	5%	2%	2%
Medical doctors	13	38	38	7	3	1
Engineers	8	38	44	3	1	6
College teachers	9	33	43	7	2	6
Bankers	8	31	50	7	1	3

(*Religion in America* 1979-1980, p. 61. The first five are cited from a list of 20 professions.)

George Gallup, director of the American Institute of Public Opinion, evaluating citizens' confidence in a variety of institutions, including religious institutions, presents us with a similar conclusion:

"I am going to read you a list of institutions in American society. Would you tell me how much confidence you, yourself, have in each one—a great deal, quite a lot, some, or very little?" . . . . Here are the results, ranked in terms of the percentages saying they have a great deal or quite a lot of confidence in each institution.

Organized religion	65%
Banks and banking	60
The military	54
Public schools	53
Newspapers	51
U.S. Supreme Court	45
Television	38
Organized labor	38
Congress	34
Big business	32

(Minneapolis Tribune, May 6, 1979.)

It would be ever so nice to let the matter rest with these summations—but we can't. Judgments from the court of public opinion, even favorable ones, can never be final judgments for ministers or ministry—they must be challenged. Ego-need may find poll estimates personally supportive and vocationally justifying, but we cannot conscientiously take all our cues from the world. There is another—a more basic—set of instruments to deal with, namely, Christian theology and the gospel call to faith. In this very moment when the world affirms us we must still subject work and being to the eternal judge who said "Woe to you when all men speak well of you, for so their fathers did to the false prophets" (Luke 6:26).

Praise, obviously, is a mixed blessing. We need it, we need it indeed. But the world's praise is nothing without the praise of God. The query which each believer must answer daily is, "Have I become too dependent on a genial reception from the world and too detached from a radical dependence on Christ?"

If our concern in ministry is to make the gospel, Christian faith, and the church palatable to the tastes of a non-Christian citizenry, and to buttress—at the same time—our frail egos, then we are only asking the world to embrace a caricature. Of necessity we'll have to revamp education according to the postulates of "accommodationism."

If, however, in our heart of hearts we want to deal with ministry in its most serious, root, New Testament sense, then necessity is laid on us to maintain a creative tension with the world. As long as faithfulness to this purpose is what inspires public reaction, and as long as this is why pollsters applaud us, well and good! But we can take nothing for granted. We must be intentional about having prophetic and ministerial parameters determine role expectations. We cannot let them devolve from choreographed electronic church models. A serious biblical approach to ministry must honor, in first order, some Old Testament antecedents. Evaluation of these key words and categories is our point of entry.

Priest-Pastor

"Priest" is a designation which enjoyed wide usage in that portion of biblical history between Abraham and Christ. Three "priestly" strands dominate the patriarchial period: Melchizedek's, Levi's, and Aaron's.

Melchizedek is something of a mysterious figure. The assertion "he had no father or mother" doesn't suggest a supernatural origin; it means there is no genealogical listing of his parentage. A king and high priest of Salem, later Jerusalem, Abraham gives him homage and pays him tithes. Christ is called "a high priest after the order of Melchizedek."

Levi was the third son of Jacob and one of the sons who died while the family was still in Egypt. His descendants were singled out for service, first in the tabernacle, then in the temple in Jerusalem. "Levites" were those members of the tribe not of the family of Aaron.

Aaron was the oldest son of Amram and Jochebed of the tribe of Levi. He and his sons were set apart for the priesthood and consecrated by Moses. Membership in this priestly guild was hereditary.

The Old Testament priest had a double function. His first responsibility was to offer sacrifices to God in behalf of the people—though exceptions to this practice were made; e.g., the head of a household could do this as did Balaam cited in Numbers 23. In general, however, people preferred to have the ordained priests perform the service. His other responsibility, also of high importance, dealt with teaching. The priest was appointed to speak in the name of God declaring the divine will.

As Israel intensified her understanding of the transcendence of God and ritualized her religion, inordinate stress was laid on the sacrificial function. Teaching fell into gross neglect and the rise of the prophets came, in a sense, as a judgment on this priestly forfeiture. Samuel's declamation, ". . . to obey is better than sacrifice" (1 Sam. 15:22), is not a repudiation of sacrifice per se. It is a protest against the people's preoccupation with sacrifice and the abuses engendered by such preoccupation. It also implies loss of the teaching element.

No one depicts the tension more clearly than Jesus. He had little to say to the priests of his day, the Sadducees. He seems to have considered them hopeless. Yet, he was sharply critical of the Scribes and Pharisees. Why these but not the priests? Was it not because they were descendents of the prophet-teachers, because they were making oral tradition and the "letter of the law" their affection rather than the living God, and because they really represented the last hope of Israel?

The Romans razed Jerusalem in A.D. 70 and Herod's temple was part of that destruction. This was a devastating blow to the priestly orders, but not the only factor in their demise. We must include the concurrent challenge which arose with the establishment of a new covenant in Christ. Out of this covenant came the church, and out of the church came an unparalleled transition of categories: the "Old Testament priestly guild" was replaced by the "New Testament understanding of the whole church as a 'priestly community'." These people felt no need to offer sacrifices to coerce response from God; they believed that Christ had made *the* sacrifice, once for all! He changed the meaning of sacrifice for all new covenant believers.

For it is impossible that the blood of bulls and goats should take away sins. Consequently, when Christ came into the world, he said, "Sacrifices and offerings thou hast not desired, but a body hast thou prepared for me; in burnt offerings and sin offerings thou hast taken no pleasure." Then I said, "Lo, I have come to do thy will, O God. . . . by that will we have been sanctified through the offering of the body of Jesus Christ once for all." (Heb. 10:4-10)

The New Testament writers do not acknowledge a special order of priests—their reason is evident—*the whole church is meant to be a priestly community for the world.* Our Christian self-understanding hinges on this audacious fact. Every believer is member and priest in the universal priesthood, but there is no guild, no special order of those holding sacerdotal privilege. Underscore that, italicize it, print it indelibly in your mind. There are offices, "Some are called to be pastors, teachers, evangelists . . . ," but there is no special order of priests!

This concept, so central to early Christian thought, carried into the post-apostolic period. Justin Martyr, Irenaeus, Tertullian and Augustine all supported it. Less happily must we also acknowledge a reversion on the part of others to Old

Testament emphases and categories—Clement of Rome, Hippolytus, and Eusebius. The real villian in the history of hierarchical development is not, however, one of these venerable post-apostolic fathers. It is the lesser known fifth-century figure, Pseudo-Dionysius the Areopagite. His theses gave sanction to those eager to perpetuate the priestly caste and these held sway until the Reformation. He dramatically categorized things in terms of "the celestial hierarchy" and "the earthly, or ecclesiastical, hierarchy." Platonic theories of distance were also part of his scheme. In the Catholic Encyclopedia we read:

Quite characteristic is the dominant idea that the different choirs of angels are less intense in their love and knowledge of God the farther they are removed from Him, just as a ray of light or of heat grows weaker the farther it travels from its source. (Vol. V, p. 14)

The essential construct can be summarized like this: "As the angels are the lowest of the heavenly hierarchy, so the bishop is the highest of the earthly hierarchy. Therefore, as you ascend from the angels to the seraphim and finally to God, so in descending order you go down from the bishop to the priest to the lay Christian." (Class Lecture, Philip Watson, Lutheran School of Theology, Chicago, July 14, 1961.)

What we have then is a graphic two-sphere description. One sphere is occupied by a celestial hierarchy, and the other by a terrestrial hierarchy. In the earthly sphere, which is the realm of the "teaching church," gradations are made in declining fashion—bishop to priest to deacon. Still lower is "the learning church" which includes monks, people, and a class of catechumens, energumens, and penitents. And dominating the whole system is the theory of proximity. The further you were from God the less spiritual you were and the less intense God's love. Small wonder that some *became* theological despairers and psychological wrecks.

The significance of Martin Luther and the reformers in this

historical progression goes beyond any theoretical affirmation of the church as the priestly community. It was their "theology in life" overthrow of the Dionysian theses and their re-casting of the role of a pastor in the life of the church which made the Reformation a viable and powerful movement.

In contrast to "priest," what does "pastor" signify? Does pastor simply mean chief priest alongside subaltern priests? Wherein is the difference? What turns Reformation Christians off when the term "priest" is used, and what turns them on when the term "pastor" is used?

The aspect of priestliness which appears to be most abhorrent to many lay Christians and not a few clergy is the arrogation that a priest has a preferential place in the economy of God, and is capable of manipulating the divine. To contend that he can conjure in behalf of others, that he has special access to divine powers, is frighteningly close to a definition of magic. Let me give you an example of what I mean.

At the start of this century a Roman Catholic bishop from Salzburg, Austria, made the following statement:

Where in heaven is power like that of the Catholic priest? With the angels? With the Mother of God? Mary conceived Christ the Son of God in her womb and gave birth to him in the stall at Bethlehem. Indeed, but observe what happens in the holy Mass. Does not the same thing to some extent take place in this holy act under the consecrating hands of the priest? Under the forms of bread and wine, Christ becomes truly and essentially present and in similar fashion is born again. . . . He (Christ) has put the priest in his place to continue the same sacrifice which he effected. He has given him authority over his whole humanity, over his whole body. The Catholic priest is able not only to bring about his presence on the altar, shut him up in the tabernacle, distribute him for the benefit of believers; he can even present him, the incarnate Son of God, as a sacrifice for the living and the dead. Christ, the only begotten Son of the Father, through whom heaven and earth were created, who sustains the whole universe, submits here to the will of the Catholic priest. (Karl Holl, *Gesammelte Aufsätze zur Kirchengeschichte,* Vol. I, Luther Der Neubau der Sittlichkeit. Tübingen, J. C. B. Mohr, 1932, pp. 6-7.)

Lest anyone construe this to be a discrediting of present day Catholicism, or justification for holding adversarial attitudes toward Roman priests, let me hasten to say that this is *only a dated illustration* of the kind of priestly expression which repulses evangelicals. We Lutherans must confirm and compliment the changes which have been going on in that great tradition. Collegiality is the order of the day. The truth about Romans is that many of them have become more evangelical than many Protestants. They have divested themselves of much that taints the term "priest" while, paradoxically, some Reformation Christians have tended to move in the opposite direction. But "pastor" is our word, and we should pursue it. That was the vigorous counsel of the late H. Grady Davis to his students in Chicago: "You are not priests," he'd inveigh, "you are pastors! You are not manipulators of the divine—there is no magic entrusted to you."

Positively, what is "the pastor's role?" In a lecture at Michigan State University in January of 1980, Dr. William Lazareth, director of the Faith and Order Commission of the World Council of Churches, sets forth these identifying functions: "A pastor is the servant of Christ who is to

- preach with power,
- teach with competence,
- officiate with reverence,
- counsel with compassion, and
- administer with efficiency.

And he is to do these things in this order of priority."

The pastor's role is a unique role, but it is only *a* role in the ministry of the Word. Along with the people the pastor must be involved in corporate worship, partnership in service, and sharing of authority. But before we deal with the character of ministry done by the congregation, let's make explicit those things identified with the pastoral task.

A pastor must *preach with power.* This does not mean haranguing listeners with Scripture verses wrenched from context. It does mean proclaiming the lordship of the risen Christ who through his messengers addresses a human situation dominated by prejudice, avarice, anxiety, and death.

A pastor is to *teach with competence,* possessing knowledge, communicating with skill, dialoging openly; good teachers will not amateurishly dismiss the serious concerns of learners.

A pastor should *officiate with reverence,* knowing that Christain worship should lead to risk in the world, not retreat from the world. The pastor is not master of the divine, but servant of the human; not aesthetic actor, but ethical catalyst.

A pastor is mandated to *counsel with compassion,* not as "the answer-giver" but as the evoker, never violating those made vulnerable by tragedy, separation, or sickness.

A pastor is to *administer with efficiency.* Autocracy breathes the wrong spirit; one must lead the flock, not drive the herd.

In general, pastors have distinguished themselves. They have all been emancipated theologically from hierarchical preconceptions and priestly assumptions. Some have yet to be emancipated psychologically. The "priest" motif is a beguiling and powerful one, and there are those few who succumb to the passion to control.

The Office of the Pastor and the General Ministry of the Church

The Christ events marks the turning point in our understanding and use of the term "priest." From this moment on there is only one spiritual head, Jesus, the great high priest. In his body, the church, ordained and unordained alike are meant to regard themselves as spiritual equals. Those ordained are identified as pastors, and pastors have no special spirituality, and they aren't different in "being." To be ordained as a pastor does not carry the same connotations as those in force when one is ordained a priest. The pastor is called to an office —a functional office. What is an office? "Something done for another . . . a service . . . assigned service, duty, or function . . . a position of trust or authority . . . with special duties. . . ." So says *Webster's Collegiate Dictionary* (5th ed).

What says Luther? Listen to this:

> Thus there is only an outward distinction for the sake of the office to which one is called by the congregation, but before God there is no difference. And only for this reason are some individuals selected from the multitude that in place of the congregation they may bear and exercise the office which they all have, not that anyone has more authority than another. Therefore no one should rise up of himself and preach in the congregation; but out of the multitude one is to be selected and appointed, and he may be removed when it is desirable.

> But now they have invented *characteres indelebiles* (indelible marks) and prate that a deposed priest is nevertheless something different from a mere layman. They even dream that a priest can nevermore become a layman or be anything else than a priest. All this is mere talk and man-made law. (*What Luther Says*. St. Louis: Concordia, 1959. Vol. II, p. 944.)

The Encyclopedia of the Lutheran Church reiterates the functional character of pastoral ministry:

Pastor, Ordination of

Ordination is the solemn act of the church designating as ministers of the Gospel, and committing to them the holy office of the Word and Sacraments, certain ones who have been regularly called by God through the church to serve in a specific field or sphere of duty. By it the church publicly acknowledges the essential need and functional character of the office of the . . . ministry (Vol. III p. 1857).

Both references plainly state that in order to occupy the pastoral office one must be called by the church, i.e., either congregation or denomination. "Call" is yet another word requiring definition. Failures to differentiate between "the call to faith" and "the formal call of the church to serve in a special place" only leads to confusion, even conflict. All Christians are, as Luther says, "called by the Holy Spirit through the Gospel." This "call to faith" is in itself "the call to be a part of the total ministry of the church."

But *how* to be selected for an office in this ministry and *where* to serve are decisions which must be made in context and must involve the judgment of peers. Assessment of personal capabilities and evaluation by fellow members is a critical part of the calling process. In reference to the *pastoral office,* e.g., Luther insists that "no one should rise up of himself and preach . . . but out of the multitude one is to be selected. . . ." Our church has never relinquished its corporate right to " . . . commit . . . the . . . office . . . to . . . certain ones . . . to serve in a specific field or sphere of duty." This is to say "the call of the church" does not emerge from individual prerogative, claim, or revelation. Pastors, among others, compound existing confusion when they profess to have "a special call," as though God has a unique plan and an extraordinary intention for them which elevates them above unordained Christians.

The Pietist tradition, a strong element in our history, gave great impetus to the idea of "God calling." The "call in the heart" was considered paramount. This generally was interpreted to mean "the call to faith" and signified "the inner call" as distinguished from "the outer call." There is no reason to quarrel with that. It only becomes a problem when individuals want to say more than "the Holy Spirit has brought me to faith in Jesus," when they claim inner revelations directing them to "*the* holy ministry," in contrast to the general ministry, and then to places of choice like Minneapolis, Seattle or the Hawaiian Islands.

The "outer call" is through the church. It is a request of persons to serve in "specific fields or spheres of duty." The fact that fallible people have a hand in it does not discredit it. We believe God works through people; yet, humility and a Christian view of human nature require us to admit that colleagues' discernment of God's will is not absolute—nor is ours. Human judgment can be clouded by a multitude of things—evasion, ambition, avarice, need, despair. Calls to places always have the mark of tentativeness upon them—but this is no cynical comment. Such calls must in fact be taken with great seriousness, particularly in this moment of history when claims of special revelation have become commonplace.

Back to the general ministry of the church and those persons who have not been ordained to the pastoral office, what should be said in their behalf? The fundamental thing to underscore, and underscore again, is the conception of the whole church as a priestly, serving community. Ordained and unordained together constitute Christ's ministry to the world. It is a ministry of the Word, and the whole church must hear that Word. But here is where things grow complex—as W. A. Visser 't Hooft says in *The Wretchedness and Greatness of the Church:* "It follows inevitably that each parishioner must be given the opportunity of entering into fellowship with his brethren who hear it with him" (p. 42). His wartime logic was spelled out in this way:

For a long time there have been only two forms of Christian activity on the part of the ordinary member—to join one of the societies attached to the parish . . . or to be one of the Parish Council which is concerned almost entirely with administrative matters. In other words, apart from the pastors, no one had the chance to exercise a true ministry in the parish. . . . Are there lay folk who can perform true ministries? Certainly, and it is happening. . . . ordinary members of the parish preach, administer the sacraments, teach the catechumens, visit the people.

And the parish does not suffer. On the contrary, it renews its life (Ibid pp. 37-38).

Without qualification, Visser 't Hooft's homogenization of roles only heightens confusion and tension between those in the pastoral office and the many who constitute the unordained ministry of the church. Ordinarily Lutherans give ready assent to "lay participation" in teaching catechumens and visiting people. But our convictions regarding the office of pastor signals some caution in how lay persons are to be encouraged to share preaching or sacramental duties.

We can only uphold the integrity of the pastoral office when we honor it as a legitimate leadership function in the general ministry of the church. Conversely, we can only uphold the general ministry of the church when we oppose its total co-option by those who occupy clerical offices. There is only one LAOS and one ministry. The ordained have an office in that ministry. They do not have "a holy ministry" and the unordained "an unholy ministry."

Laos is the term encompassing all the people of God, ordained and unordained—ministry applies to all, "clerical" and "lay."

Being or Doing?—Implications for Pastors and Parishioners

Ever since the Reformation, most Lutherans have tried to avoid a bifurcation in the orders of "being," or "experience." A few contrariwise, have wanted to legitimize a two-tiered distinction after the manner of Pseudo-Dionysius, and they have ready company in all who wish to perpetuate clerical/lay distinctions in spirituality. But pastors do not have, innately, a different *esse* (being) nor are they infused at ordination with a different *esse*. They are called to an office for the *bene esse*—the well being—of both church and world.

This word *esse* (Latin for "being,") needs further comment.

People in our day use it in an ontological sense looking for qualities and virtues resident in human nature or bestowed on human nature. So, in the language of the street, certain persons are said to be endowed with special attributes which qualify them for roles like "pastor." Kindness, meekness, long-suffering, etc. are considered innate and made the basis of selection. Theorists of this persuasion say, "St. Paul referred to these things," which indeed he did, but he saw them as fruits of the Spirit and characteristics applicable to all Christians.

The medieval church made a great deal more of bestowed character. "Infusion" was its big word. It taught that what a candidate for the priesthood didn't have innately was imparted through the sacrament of ordination. The priest was given "an indelible character." It was his forever. This is what Luther railed against. He initiated a radical redefinition of the pastoral office based not on "being" but on "doing," and this should surprise no one. Luther's referrent was Christ. It was he who called tax-collectors, foul-mouthed fishermen, even a religious bigot from Tarsus, to be his disciples and apostles—if you will, his first pastors. Theologically we say "He knew what was in man" but it was the Hebrew mandate "to do" rather than the Greek injunction "to be" which marked the direction of the Master's ministry. Philosophically this squares with John Macmurray's thesis ". . . that if we start from the 'I think' there is no possibility of arriving at action; whereas it is possible to derive the theoretical from the practical if we affirm the primacy of action" (*The Self as Agent*, p. 165).

Preaching, teaching, officiating, counseling, administrating, constitute our acting, our doing. These things are not mere palliatives for congregations or church bodies fighting for survival. They are for the body of Christ what eating, sleeping, thinking, and exercising are for every human creature. We're dependent on them as life-support elements for as long as we live. A pastor shares "the Bread of life" and "the Water of life" from the pulpit; teaching centers in him who is "the Truth"; officiating is not an act of sacrifice—it points to him who is "the Sacrifice"; caring is modeled after "the Good Shepherd." Christ's undershepherd is ". . . to seek the lost . . . combat heresy . . . show fatherly mercy to those entrusted to him . . . liberate them from guilt. . . ." (*Theological Dictionary of the New Testament*, Vol. VI, p. 498). Finally, a pastor is to administrate in the spirit of Him who said, "You know that those who are supposed to rule over the Gentiles lord it over them. . . . But it shall not be so among you." (Mark 10: 42-43) Our conclusion? "It is thus the nature of an agent to act not in terms of his own nature, but in terms of the nature of the object, that is, of the Other" (*The Self as Agent*, p. 168). For us this means Christ.

A pastor is to be a doer, the trained theologian called by the church to preach and teach. But the pastor is only one in a whole ministerial priesthood which is to function "pastorally." Therefore pastors should not arrogate everything to themselves. They should understand that it is as though the church has placed a one-person seminary faculty in each congregation to train and lead the people in ministering. But all of this raises serious questions: "Is it self defeating for pastors to think this broadly and function in a shared ministry? Will they suffer consequent loss of status as leaders and theologians?" Ernst Käsemann makes a noteworthy response:

Now, I am a theologian myself and intend to remain one, so this danger cannot possibly be as great as may appear at first sight. But everything depends on giving ministry and ministries their proper place. They can never be something external to, and imposed upon, the general body of disciples, but always a specific concrete realization of its life. But if we are to understand this process aright we must first of all be clear that, while discipleship is commanded for all, yet the content of its doing and becoming is never the same for all. (*New Testament Questions for Today*, p. 291).

In this context and with these qualifications Visser 't Hooft's comments about ordinary members' ministry *in* the church can be given proper consideration. Teaching? Yes! Visiting? Yes! Preaching and Sacrament sharing? With qualification. Parishioners should not be summarily excluded. Pastors of this generation have found good things happening as they learned to use congregational members in the worship life of the church. Participants, however, should be trained for particular roles and this elementary distinction must be imbedded in their consciousness: the worship of the *laos*, the people of God, is not the same as the ministry of the *laos*. Luther reminds us that ". . . the diaconate (Christian service) is not . . . reading the Gospel or Epistle, . . . but the ministry of distributing the Church's alms to the poor." We should not confuse ministry with worship, i.e., listening to sermons, reading lessons, or assisting with communion. More explicitly, ministry ought not have its point of emphasis "*in* the church" but "*out* in the world." Fairness to Visser 't Hooft demands that we recognize his awareness of that too.

Like Käsemann, I am not about to abandon the pastoral office or give up its prerogatives, but fulfilling it doesn't mean that "I" have to do everything. The extended seminary faculty concept persists—we are there to inspire, witness, train, lead, teach, and serve. We must find ways of including fellow members in ritual, teaching, and service. And the major hurdle is not methodology—it is "the will" of the pastor. Pastors must "will" participation, not out of expediency or duress, but out of a magnanimity which aids people in ministering. They must resist the ego exercise of doing the ministry for them. This should neither demean office nor diminish person. But with such caring and sharing, caution!

It is a disfavor to all to invite unknowing and untrained people, however zealous, to officiate from the pulpit or in the classroom and then be chagrined by discourses which reek of heresy, self-justification, or some form of desiccated humanism. It is equally bad to handle sacraments in an indiscriminate way. The pastoral *office* exists primarily to keep proclamation centered on the Gospel, secondarily to keep it from falling into mere moralism. It exists to have the sacraments rightly administered and to keep sacramental observances from degenerating into magic.

The broader questions of ministry, *beyond* life in the congregation, are still to be dealt with. If we complain that preoccupation with ritual inside the church can divert ethically responsible action, we must also contend that good worship can and should lead to ministerial effectiveness outside of the church. Worship of God should free us so we can ". . . be priests for others," and recognize "what God doesn't need, the neighbor does. . . ." The challenge is not to get people to serve the church, but to get the church to serve the world—more on that in the section on *The Role of the Congregation in the Exercise of Ministry.* At this juncture it is enough to confess the painful truth that each of us has a long, long way to go. Pastors and people are only disciples, learners. Continuing development is in order for both pew and pulpit.

A Performance Check

How realistic have we been? Are we asking too much from church people or not nearly enough? Are there not immense areas of potential growth in both the worship life and the wider ministry of the *laos?* And what of those to whom the pastoral office is committed? Is the expectation too great or too little? Have we even desired the right things of our pastors? Have they required the essential things of themselves?

Some pastors say they'd like to spend more time preparing sermons; they'd like to devote more attention to spiritual formation (the term "piety" which has greater ethical implication and less mystical inference is preferable); they want to be better family members. In the same breath much of this is deferred because of "other concerns." Are those "other concerns" primary concerns of the parishioners and the rest of the world, or have they become the escape hatch for those beleaguered by self-doubt, non-commitment to essential elements in the pastor's role, and the wear and tear of life in western culture?

Only God can give the ultimate word, but we return—full cycle—to some penultimate human checks. Two instruments tell us a great deal about the church, its pastors and its constituent members. One is a study conducted by the Lutheran Church in America and entitled *Growth in Ministry* (Fortress, 1979). The other is Search Institute's *Ten Faces of Ministry* (Augsburg, 1979). What do these probes reveal? Observe!

Growth in Ministry: The Lutheran Church in America and the Lutheran Church-Missouri Synod were partners in this project, which began in 1973. The American Lutheran Church was also related to the program. . . . Some 400 pastors, 260 spouses, and 2,950 lay members contributed to the basic research.

Six pastoral roles have been discovered operating in the thinking of lay leaders, pastors, and pastors' wives. . . . listed in order of the importance of the roles:

1. The Pastor as Priest and Preacher . . . .
2. The Pastor's Personal and Spiritual Development . . . .
3. The Pastor as Organizer . . . .
4. The Pastor as Teacher and Visitor . . . .
5. The Pastor's Community and Social Involvement . . . .
6. The Pastor as Office Administrator . . . .

. . . . pastors consistently rate their effectiveness lower than they are rated by lay members of their congregations, and by their spouses. One pastor in the project explained this by saying, "When members say *effective*, they think *faithful*. When pastors say *effective*, they think *perfect*." More open communication between pastor and people may help pastors to more realistic understandings of their own effectiveness."

Ten Faces of Ministry: The product of Search Institute which also engaged in extensive research—5000 Lutherans—identified the preferred status of Five Ministry Skills:

1. Community Through Word and Sacraments . . . .
2. Making Ministry of Administration . . . .
3. Ministry of Counseling . . . .
4. Reaching Out with Compassion . . . .
5. Informed Leadership of Liturgical Worship . . . .

The studies are valuable and strikingly similar, but there is reason to believe that Lutherans have long known, in their hearts, what these projects with computer help now confirm. We seem to be on target. Congregational members appear to have more realistic expectations of pastors than pastors realize, just as the world outside of the church ascribes a greater credibility to Christian leaders than they assume for themselves. Even when pastors and congregations aren't performing as well as they can, the're still in a credible position and things could brighten immeasurably with increased devotion to those essential tasks.

So we move, inexorably, toward a definition of ministry, and we ought not be discouraged by the fact that we have not yet found a fully satisfying one, or given the ones we have adequate expression. That must never deter ministering to the world. We know what the components are, and this dialectic is meant to spur execution more than to give final explanation.

2 THE PASTOR/PEOPLE PARTNERSHIP

One New Testament epistle that exemplifies the best in pastor-people relationships is Paul's letter to the church at Philippi. Interpreters have long talked about this as Paul's beloved congregation. The Philippians caused little trouble. Their care for him was extra special. He comments gratefully:

I thank my God in all my remembrance of you, always in every prayer of mine for you all making my prayer with joy . . . , thankful for your partnership in the gospel from the first day until now. And I am sure that he who began a good work in you will bring it to completion at the day of Jesus Christ. It is right for me to feel thus about you all, because I hold you in my heart. . . . (Phil. 1:3-7).

His great personal gratitude, however, is not the thing I want to deal with. Out of the profuse thanks in both the opening and closing chapters, a special word captures attention and bids for the position of prominence: partnership!

It was kind of you to share my trouble. And you Philippians yourselves know that in the beginning of the gospel, when I left Macedonia, no church entered into partnership with me in giving and receiving except you only; for even in Thessalonica you sent me help once and again. Not that I seek the gift: but I seek the fruit which increases to your credit. I have received full payment, and more; I am filled, having received from Epaphroditus the gifts you sent, a fragment offering, a sacrifice acceptable and pleasing to God (Phil. 4:14-18).

"Partnership" is a translation of the Greek term *koinonia*.

35

What brings this partnership into being? What are its basic elements? Paul makes clear that it has to do with the gospel. But the gospel is the proclamation of a yet more basic something, and this basic something is what Jesus Christ has done for Paul and for all of us. To put it another way, Paul and his Philippian friends are united in something done for them. They manifest that unity even further in their common telling of what was done. The root message is always there: Jesus died for Paul; Jesus died for you; Jesus died for me. And he rose on the third day for all of us. The unity of his act and the timeless application of the fact is constant.

God's favor to him and his special place among the apostles notwithstanding, no hierarchical exclusiveness is generated in Paul. He claims no spiritual superiority. To the contrary, he uses a most egalitarian term, "yokefellow," to describe relationships. Occasionally accused by moderns of being sexist, he even calls the bickering women Euodia and Syntiche his "fellow-workers . . . who have labored side by side with me in the Gospel." Under a yoke one does not have preeminence over another. They work together, pull together, share the burden and heat of the day together.

This sense of partnership is a vital necessity in the life of the modern church. We do not maximize it as a possibility if we have an over-riding commitment to hierarchical structures. We do maximize it if we actualize the priesthood of all believers. But what if we don't have this sense of partnership, or what if we have it in an unsatisfactory way? How can we have it, yet not have it? The answer, I believe, lies in constricting myths which impair relationships in the church. They are often subtle, but real, and each is a negative factor.

Myths Held by Pastors that Impede Partnership

The first of these myths has its origin in training circumstances where well-intentioned but badly mistaken professors or intern supervisors tell theological charges: *It is best never to get too close to your parishioners.* The consequences are devastating. Objectivity in counseling is probably a major reason for giving this advice, but the net effect is that some have never gotten "too close" to their parishioners; they haven't gotten to them at all. Someone will probe, "what kind of closeness are you talking about, social or psychological?" I'm not sure we can neatly separate "kinds," but I'm talking about that quality of identification which risks full involvement, which evokes the utmost trust and confidence. This may or may not start with social engagement, but it is more than mere socializing.

Perhaps Axel-Ivar Berglund says it best. Here is a Lutheran pastor of the Church of Sweden who is devoting his ministry to the people of South Africa. Identifying with the native black population, his work has been difficult and his life filled with tragedy. Yet, hear what he said while lecturing in Florida in March, 1980:

Clinical coolness or a standing aloof of the deepest sentiment in all men is everything but the divine ministry authorized by Him whose most profound characteristic is love!

A minister "up there," far out of reach, or snugly tucked away somewhere only to be taken out of the place of seclusion when needed, has never really had a recognized place in the church. . . . If the church is to be what it is expected to be, a minister must be in the midst of people, in their toil and their struggles for survival, with the utmost visibility. No other place other than the most exposed, most relevant and most evident is worthy of the minister of a living church!

We need to reestablish again the basic principle that nobody can help anyone without becoming involved, without entering with one's whole person into the painful situation, including the risk of becoming hurt, wounded or even destroyed in the process. This is the way that the incarnation followed, and what other more worthy example does the church and its ministry have than He who took precisely that way?

37

If pastors are to be faulted on one side or the other, it is better to fault them for over-identification rather than under-identification. The warrant for this counsel, as Pastor Berglund says, is the New Testament and its Christ, the essence of which is "salvation comes by identification." God in his infinite love does not stand apart. He was ". . . in Christ reconciling the world to himself. . . ." (2 Cor. 5:19). God takes on the flesh of this social order and makes clear beyond any shadow of doubt that his heart is love and his will is to reach into the worst of human situations and bring wholeness. His Christ does not emerge unscathed. He is mocked, physically abused, and put to death, but "salvation comes by identification."

Two bishops came to Minneapolis in the fall of 1975. One was a Lutheran from Europe, the other a Roman Catholic from South America. The European said, in effect, "We must stop this talk about social involvement and get back to preaching the gospel." He received a standing ovation. The bishop from South America in stark contrast said, "We must emulate our Lord Jesus Christ and be dirtied and bruised by association with the scorned and disenfranchised." Applause for him was moderate. Yet, identification with others is the key; and in a world where salt-of-the-earth people want little more than for a pastor to love them, share a portion of life with them, stand with them in temptation, sorrow and pain— it is counterproductive to tell those pastors, "It is best never to get too close to parishioners."

A second myth impeding partnership is that *parishioners are incapable of theological reflection.* Is this anything other than an expression of intellectual arrogance? That the theological leader is a unique creature endowed with capacities for understanding nuances and mysteries beyond the grasp of the common person is a delusion. Such mistaken superiority seeks vindication in a variety of ways, even using Martin

Luther to support its bias. It is said that attitudinally, if not in content, he helped create such a climate. Two factors may be noted as partial explanations: first, Luther's hatred of anything smacking of sophistry; second, his explicit criticism of the laity for unrepentant libertinism and his implicit doubt regarding their reflective ability. But we must still come out strongly on Luther's behalf. He really didn't deprecate his hearers; extended reading bears this out. A balanced critique will show that he didn't want anything to interfere with people's belief in the Gospel or the plain truth of Christ. Adaptability to hearers was part of his preaching genius.

Let us remember, however, that this is not the sixteenth century. Many who worship in our churches are university trained. The level of sophistication is much higher. While Luther did not want the sophisticated concerns of a few to diminish proclamation for many, do we not have to think of that conversely and make sure we don't lose our audience by a simplistic dealing with the gospel in an age of great complexity?

Is "theological reflection" in our congregations less than excellent? If the answer is yes, why is it yes? Is it because people lack ability to hear and perceive, or is it because preachers lack willingness to challenge and teach? One of the best scholars in the church spent a week on retreat with sixty lay persons from a west coast community. Mill-wrights, lumberjacks, and commercial fishermen came together to study basic Lutheran documents including the Augsburg Confession. Were they capable of theological reflection? "One of the most exciting and perceptive groups I've ever worked with," said the professor. Only intellectual pride and a patronizing stance allows the thesis, "Keep sermons shallow and teaching tame." One might even devilishly think that this could be license for clerical laziness.

Pastors must hold good estimates and expectations of lay colleagues. They must hold them of themselves. We must do away with this I'm-no-theologian—I'm-only-a-pastor excuse-making. The primary role of the pastor is that of theologian. Karl Barth's laudatory statement on Schleiermacher says something to all of us:

We cannot be mindful enough of the fact that Schleiermacher was not one of those theologians who are in the habit, under some pretext or other, of dissociating themselves from the most difficult and decisive theological situation, that in which the theologian, without security of any kind, must prove himself solely as a theologian. I refer to the situation of the man in the pulpit. Schleiermacher did not only not avoid this most exposed position, but actually sought it, throughout his life, as the place for his "own office." He sought it "with enthusiasm", as one of his friends avowed in 1804, almost with astonishment. (*Protestant Theology in the Nineteenth Century,* pp. 429f.)

The third myth eddying in pastors' minds is: *ministry would be better elsewhere.* What a debilitating thing this is for partnership. Such pastors may be physically among their people but psychologically they are in dysfunction. They have projected themselves into greener pastures. What can ensue other than diminished appreciation for current circumstances and a diminished expectation of those with whom they are supposed to minister? This attitude cannot be hidden; it will leak out. Small wonder then that present partners draw back, exhibit reticence, and are less demonstrative in their affection for pastoral leadership. Not only are we tempted to overestimate other places and positions—larger, future, more affluent ones; we undercut and fail to do justice to ministry potential where we are.

All myths gusting around in the church do not, however, come from the ranks of the clergy. Some originate with the laity.

Myths Held by Parishioners that Impede Partnership

Perhaps the most grating of all lay myths is that *there is a double standard, one for pastors and one for parishioners.*

Seldom is this openly stated, but it can hardly be dismissed as inconsequential in the lives of parsonage people. Whatever distress it causes the pastor and the pastors' spouse, it is demonic in the way it impacts the lives of the pastor's children. "Did you hear about the pastor's son? . . . I saw the reverend's daughter . . . etc." A special onus sits on them because they are parsonage youngsters.

Some very sensitive studies are needed on the children of professional people. We cannot blindly defend bizarre behavior or sins they share with their peers, but if we want to understand them we must see the exaggerated and terrible tensions they live in. It's a conflict situation through and through. At home, even in the most modest of parsonages and with the most considerate parents, there is an anticipated level of morality, an anticipated commitment of faith. Outside the home some exaggerate this normal expectation and turn it into an abnormal one. It's not just Christian conviction versus secular culture; it's an unwarranted expectation of Christian perfectionism versus culture.

Meanwhile—in the school, on the playground, at work— other forces are in operation. They are the dynamics of a secular culture. The preacher's kid is caught; he or she seeks love and security at home, but he or she also wants the approbation of peers in the world. What torment! "Do I stay within the circle of parental affection and support their values, or do I enter the circle of my companions in the world and seek commendation from them?" Over-reaction from "rebels" to prove that they are one of the crowd often hurts them— even as it hurts their parents—but if a P. K. doesn't test freedom as a youth, he or she will end up doing it as an adult. Obviously we anticipate growth; obviously we do not want to avoid a necessary tension between Christian and culture. But we do need to be sensitive to those who are expected to be something more or "better" than the rest.

Well, you say, shouldn't the pastor and his family be an

example? To which I must answer, yes. However, neither the pastor nor the children should be held accountable to other people's "perfectionist standards," it's bad enough when they create their own. "Love God and love the neighbor"—is the ethical imperative laid on parsonage people, and all others in the priesthood of all believers.

Another of those unspoken but real myths: *If the church isn't growing it's the pastor's fault.* Such an assertion does not ordinarily flare into open criticism until those in the pew want a change, but for pastors it is a nagging day-by-day guilt item. The flaw in the myth is that the responsibility for evangelizing rests with the pastor. Like all myths, it contains a partial truth. Some of the responsibility does belong to the pastor, but not all. It is also fair to say that pastors have been known to invert this, contending that "the responsibility belongs to parishioners." Both are wrong. Partnership is right. Pastors must "lead people in ministering" and people must "share in that ministering." A pastor's task is to clarify what the gospel is; he or she must demonstrate zeal for the furtherance of the gospel; he or she must share the scandal of the cross. But there is no reason to feel that the pastor must do these things alone, and there is absolutely no reason for parishioners to think that "all we have to do is sit back and either applaud or decry our pastor's efforts."

A third myth: *The church has slipped because pastors have been demythologizing the Bible.* The obvious reference is to movements and methods generated by the work of Rudolf Bultmann. He is the central figure in the "interpretation storm." Using modern tools of interpretation, employing "the historical-critical method," he sought to get behind words and forms and back to the original meaning of the text. Little have people realized the naivete they are party to. Now some are shaken by the use of the term "demythologizing." If they hear that there may well have been two authors of Isaiah, or that the first chapters of Genesis were a later addition, or that Matthew's life of Christ was influenced by churchly concerns, they are ready to conclude that such teaching undermines the authority of Scripture and the authority for faith. But does it? Where is their center of trust? Is it simply in a literalistic understanding of the Bible?

No uncritical defense should be made of Bultmann, but neither should we allow unknowning detractors to slander him and tar his efforts with a bad brush. They think he worshiped the scientific method and destroyed appreciation for the holy writings. In actuality he underscored the limitations of that method and emphasized the indispensability of the Scriptural Word. Look at what he says:

> Thus there can be no question of discarding historical criticism. But we must understand its true significance. It is needed to train us for freedom and veracity—not only by freeing us from a specific traditional conception of history, but because it frees us from bondage to every historical construction which is within the scope of historical science, and brings us to the realization that the world which faith wills to grasp is absolutely unattainable by means of scientific research.

> What is really asked is whether we are willing to hear the answer that we are sinners and must accept grace. We are questioned the more forcibly, the more our history in general is characterized by those 'experiences' in the intercourse of *I* and *Thou;* but with still greater force when that history includes the encounter with the *Thou* which is qualified by Christian faith and Christian love—that is, the more we stand within the history of the Christian church.

> 'The more' is required, for today it no longer seems possible to say simply *that* we stand within the church. For where is the Christian church? Where is the Word proclaimed? But even if we really had to say that the Christian church has vanished, it would still be no less possible to believe the Word of Scripture (which at least exists as a 'printed book'); for certainly the law cannot vanish. And thus it would be possible for the Christian church to arise again. (*Faith and Understanding*, Vol. I, pp. 31, 141, 143.)

Are these the words of a destroyer? What Bultmann is really getting at is that God is not subject to the scientific method either to validate his presence or eradicate it.

It would be dishonest to say that modern study hasn't affected some church members adversely. It has. Yet if they would stop for a moment and really look at the situation, maybe they would understand that they have been freed to deal with the real object of faith—Christ himself.

Let me propose a different challenge. I suggest that we turn our critical faculties loose on demythologizing *practice*. The corruption that runs amok in this hour is the corruption of the practice of theology. We've been reviewing myths which impede partnership, myths of the clergy, myths of the laity. Shouldn't we *de myth* the "working" myths of both?

The thing that makes belief in any myth dangerous is that it contains an element of truth. To demythologize means to get behind the myth to the real issue. So, in summation, here's what I suggest the real issues are:

- love identification between pastor and people
- parishioners' ability to learn and pastors' willingness to teach
- devotion to one's call to serve, and the taming of ambition
- the need for example and the exposure of hypocrisy in "expecting things of others you don't expect of yourself"
- whose task it is to evangelize
- the elimination of scapegoats and coming to grips with good practice.

In contrast to myths which impede partnership, what elements work positively for good relations?

Acts that Enhance Partnership

What can we really do to induce the kind of partnership that St. Paul talked about? The first answer is obvious, *Give assistance in circumstances of distress.* This can be done long-range, like from America to Africa, but some of the most productive expressions of help come from first-hand personal interaction. God could have loved from afar, and did, but he sent his Son into the world. Incarnation is not simply an element of theology to be debated; it is a reality to be cherished. God already knows what we are only struggling to know, viz., "Salvation does come by identification." Only by intimate association and loving is there a gospel, a good word for the sinner, the outcast, the diseased, the imprisoned, the estranged. Personal involvement is axiomatic.

There is real partnership in congregational life, fellowship that is truly redemptive. Are congregations at times unduly critical of pastors and pastors' spouses and pastors' children? Yes, indeed. But there are also tremendously moving accounts of how people in our parishes have accepted a pastor's pregnant, unwed daughter; stood with their wayward sons; and in very fact loved them and their distraught parents back into wholeness of life. Assistance in distress—whether it originates with the pastor or people—surely enhances partnership.

Much harder, in a way, is *being an advocate for the oppressed*. Who pleads their cause? Who speaks, as James says, "for the fatherless and widow?" Who is advocate for black brothers and sisters, Latins, Asians, Native Americans? Where are those who cry out for the poor? Who speaks for prisoners and against prison conditions? Why, in the year of the child, were so many children disinherited? If the church is to maintain its credibility, it cannot but speak and act in behalf of such people. Christians must be advocates.

Will such efforts imperil present relationships with the affluent, the middleclass, the Caucasian world? They might. But that isn't the issue. The issue is Christian obedience to love God and love the neighbor. If associates sever relationships because we love, they were not root partners in the first place. Our standing with the affluent is not the risk—our standing before God is.

Finally, the most common act that enhances partnership is

association in worship and service. So, pastors, do you in priestly fashion do it for them, or, inviting participation, do it with them? To reiterate, I am not suggesting that the one called to the pastoral office indiscriminately abandon pulpit and classroom anymore than I am suggesting that others presumptuously usurp those posts. The pastor is the theologian-in-residence, the trained preacher, the orchestrator of the church's worship life; but there are all kinds of ways to invite responsible participation. Worship stimulation has come by member participation. The same is true of service.

I think that pastors have won the hearts of people, not only as Paul said by being yoked together in the proclamation of the gospel, but, by helping them combine grain, put up cement blocks, package relief items, cut the hair of invalids. These acts, along with sound teaching and lucid sermonizing, create an amazing solidarity. There should be no neglect of mandated responsibilities, but people do love to see their pastor involved in the common ventures of life.

The partnership which blossoms from serving together is a tremendous force for good. Risks taken and energies shared are welding elements in all human relationships.

It was a University of Michigan sociology professor who gave added impetus to this thesis for many pastors. He had a multitude of stimulating insights. One has particular application here: "Fellowship emerges from working together." "When you try to have fellowship for the sake of fellowship," he said, "it tends to degenerate into amusement for amusement's sake. All this grows hackneyed and people weary of it." The professor was and is right. Work together produces partnership. Paul's kind words to Philippian friends underscores that. There is not only stimulation of the heart; there is a binding of hearts.

I remember the infamous year 1929 from childhood. In the parsonage there were hushed conversations. A church building was under construction and there was talk of "foreclosing on a mortgage." Council members came and went—worried people, worried talk. One evening they counted the biggest pile of pennies, nickels, and dimes I had ever seen. Savings had been dredged from everywhere. The coins were wrapped and laid in a suitcase. It took two men to carry that case to John Bain's bank. The event was never forgotten. Today there is still fond recollection and soft conversation about what had been lived through together. Some partners are deceased, but not even death can break the bond of fellowship forged in work done side by side.

Where does all of this lead us? To cynicism about the church's future? To anti-clericism or anti-laicism? To a point of immobility? Not at all. It offers an avenue to freer, more wholesome, and more intimate relationships. It offers the chance to know better where the clergy and laity are coming from and where the whole *laos* of God should be going.

3 THE ROLE OF THE SEMINARY IN THE PREPARATION OF PASTORS

The designation is seminary, not theological school, and the difference is deliberate. "Seminary" signifies, with intention, an institution of the church whose purpose is to prepare pastors for leadership roles in the lives of constituent congregations. "Theological school" is a less intimate term which may or may not signify close churchly ties and such purposeful intent.

In days past "theological school" frequently depicted a learning center highly academic and theoretical in character. "Seminary" denoted something more practical. Its reputation was that of being professional, functional. Critics uncharitably even labeled seminaries "trade schools." ALC seminaries have never been that. In actuality, they modeled their style and curriculum according to northern European graduate school design, and now, ironically, receive double criticism. Some say they are not sufficiently academic; others say they are not sufficiently practical.

It would be a tragedy to pander to those who see theological education as "pure knowledge." Americans studying in Germany are often anxiety-stricken with the accusation that they are . . . shallow theologically, mere functionalists, Fundamentalist in orientation, and bereft of more esoteric abilities. The alternative—pandering to the functionalists—would not only be tragedy; it would be disaster. The heresies that

49

plague us today are largely functional heresies. Ergo, our seminaries stand between theory and practice endeavoring to be intellectually responsible and practically sensitive without having to make the false choice of either-or.

One thing is certain: seminaries are not just retreat centers for theological pedants. They are training centers to prepare pastors for leadership roles in congregations. Whatever differences exist between the respective Lutheran church bodies, each of them sees church and seminaries in

An Interdependent Relationship

It is axiomatic that the church and its seminaries live in a mutually dependent and beneficial relationship. By analogy, it is the kind of relationship St. Paul describes between the body and its respective parts in 1 Corinthians 12:14-20.

For the body does not consist of one member but of many. If the foot should say, "Because I am not a hand, I do not belong to the body," that would not make it any less a part of the body. . . . If all were a single organ, where would the body be? As it is, there are many parts, yet one body.

The body is the corporate entity; organs are essential parts. Without them bodily function is impaired and life may even be threatened.

Seminaries are vital organs in the church's life, but they are organs. If they are sick or weak, the whole church will reflect their sickness or weakness. If the rest of the church is sick or weak, that conversely will have its effect on the seminaries. The comparison also holds for health. Healthy parts suggest a healthy whole; a healthy whole suggests healthy parts.

Paul's intention is to describe the body, the church. Our analogy is appropriate only insofar as seminaries represent the teaching function and office. But the situational challenge is to deal deliberately with the realities—namely, the denominations and the seminaries we are vitally involved with. Let us make our first approach from a seminary perspective, then reverse ourselves and see things from a broader, churchly perspective. What we will discover in the process is a love relationship par excellence.

The sensitivity of the seminaries to the church

The first thing for pastoral training centers to recognize is their purpose and function in the wider context. Awareness of its subordinate role will diminish and allay any seminary's temptation to be an entity concerned only with its own life.

Institutions are much akin to people. They take on a character all their own. Like human beings, they too are affected by sin. They can become frighteningly self-centered and manifest the alarming fact that their corporate direction is centripetal. When concerned alumni and institutional regents reflect on this, they must do more than piously wring their hands lamenting a slide toward ingrownness and the perpetuating of the institutional self for the sake of the self. Confession must become corporate repentance and corporate repentance means returning to the mandated role wherein the organ properly serves the body.

"Serving the body" is the general intention and the prevailing motif in Lutheran seminary situations. There is high concern to honor the servant role. Seminary people are very sensitive to the moods and concerns of the church, and not for the base reason that the church subsidizes them financially. There is truly a Christian desire to have the church be effective in its ministry to the world.

Seminary people are like each of us, "saint and sinner." No one wants to "sweep their sins under the rug," but it is time to vocalize support and say some laudatory things in their behalf for they are, by and large, highly motivated people. Each has evidenced commitment to Christ, to the gospel, to God's revelation, to Scripture's role and function in the church, to a life of service.

It is easy to recall occasions in which tensions between "mother" church and "daughter" institutions warranted review and correction. In the last decade, e.g., the American Lutheran Church reasserted its concern that academically precocious people—if they wished to teach—have meaningful practical parish experience. Our church has always wanted to combine professorial excellence with legitimate pastoral congregational experience. Such thinking, however, is not limited to our denomination. Karl Barth, titan of the Reformed tradition, had strong commitments to this thesis. His biographer, Eberhard Busch, wrote:

> He was concerned . . . to supervise the progress of a sound younger generation of theological scholars. . . . But he never forgot that the future task of the theological student was usually work in the pastorate—indeed his instruction was primarily oriented in that direction. Furthermore, he also wanted this practical task to be the presupposition of those who aimed to be theological scholars and teachers. He thought that people would notice "at every turn if these would-be teachers had never made 'the kerygma' to which there was so much appeal, their own responsibility, if they had never presented it in its canonical Old and New Testament form, with humility and patience, with delight and love, in preaching, instruction and pastoral work, serving a real community, instead of always just thinking *about* it and talking *about* it. . . ." (*Karl Barth*, p. 353.)

In 1978 the Church Council of The American Lutheran Church affirmed the policy of the Board for Theological Education and Ministry "requiring parish experience as a prerequisite for seminary faculty positions." ALC seminary representatives in concert with others produced a document, "Appointment, Reappointment, Termination, Dismissal, and Tenure for The American Lutheran Church Seminary Faculties," which was adopted as our working policy. The key portion bearing on parish experience reads:

The Church Council of The American Lutheran Church requires three years of parish experience before an ordained faculty member can be considered for tenure in a seminary of this church. The board affirms this policy as its ordinary expectation before the granting of tenure.

Over and over again daughter seminaries demonstrate sensitivity to the parent body. Professors are in the forefront as the churches most devoted and ardent supporters. They are also among the most conscientious critics. This necessitates a statement on institutional integrity: Seminaries, being organs of the church, are not mere mouth organs or puppets for one part or all of the bureaucracy. They do not identify the corporate church as ultimate master; they heed rather the church's Christ and their Christ. He is head of the whole body. The church is the seminary's mother—not her master. As part of the whole ministering community, seminaries share the "priestly function" of bringing solace and healing, giving guidance, support, and encouragement. But theirs is also a prophetic role. They sharpen and declare the whole counsel of God, judgment and grace. If the church moves on a questionable course or refuses to embark on a most proper one, then the seminaries not only should speak, they must speak.

It is important that sensitivity be two-directional; now we reverse the order.

The sensitivity of the church to the seminaries

There are people who are threatened by progressive theological education. Their lives are built on the assumption that truth has been given, once! Now the task of the believing community is simply to defend it. A big support passage for them is the frequently quoted Jude, verse 3: ". . . the faith which was once delivered to the saints." How do they interpret that? Improperly, they shift terms and displace "faith" with "theology." So, in practice, the passage reads for them,

". . . the *theology* once delivered . . ." And it is made absolute.

But let's talk about theology, not a forced interpretation of one passage. There are, of course, constants in theology, but not absolutes. Theology—at its very best—is human response to and reflection on the mighty deeds of God. It is also reflection on the faith-life response of those who constitute the believing community. As human reflection, it always has the element of tentativeness within it. Many sincere Christians do not like to be reminded of that; yet, it is an inescapable fact.

The issue is that of changing and unchanging elements. Theology as a science is in this respect no different from other sciences. There are constants, all admit, in agriculture and farming. There are basic elements, oxygen, hydrogen, nitrogen, phosphates, sun and soil. And there is produce. We have milk, meat, poultry, corn, and wheat. But who plows with mules, and how much milking is done by hand? The science of farming has changed, and agricultural science has created better agricultural produce.

Can we not admit that there are both constants and variables in theology? The science of theology also has basic elements and products. The basics have constancy, the person of God, his revelation in Christ, the cross, grace, resurrection, and the like. The variables are in the scientific treatment and growth—and the aim is better products, viz., believing people, pastors, congregations, and better forms of ministry with which the church addresses the world.

The task of a seminary faculty has always been to develop persons who can express truth and love by word and deed in the actualities of human existence. Seminary faculty persons are obligated to use the best resources available. They want their people on the cutting edge.

What happens though when a church does not—or will not —keep up with modern study? The alternatives are disturbing and counter-productive:

- it may seek, find, and worship absolutes, false absolutes;

- it may try to verify faith on experiential grounds;

- it may develop an "inquisitorial attitude" over against its institutions of learning.

Then dark days come, days of suspicion, and doubt, and accusation, and regression. The name of the game becomes "Let's Get the Intellectuals," and the war is on. It is critical for church members—lay or clergy—to consciously avoid this corrupting urge, and the only way to do it is by open-minded study.

In light of the human desire to make truth static, it is necessary to plead the cause of academic freedom in every generation. Seminaries need breathing room. The church's trust level in and sensitivity for the seminaries must be high. Nothing less will be productive. An illustration is also in order here:

In 1962 a situation arose involving the publication of a document entitled *Called to Be Human*. It was a challenging work, not written by seminary personnel, but most surely reflecting many things included in seminary teaching. The reception was mixed, for it raised basic interpretive issues.

- Was Adam a single human being, or is "Adam" a collective term representing all mankind?

- Doesn't the martyrdom of Stephen become prototypical for Christians, shouldn't we all be vulnerable like Christ?

The seminaries were traditionally sensitive to the church, but now it became critical for the church to prove its sensitivity to the seminaries. This was a watershed occasion. If the church discredited the work and beat a hasty retreat into a wooden literalism, the seminaries would be muzzled and dealt a crippling blow. At the same time, no one could ignore the anguished cries of those who had either caught—or been taught—the fevers of fundamentalism.

The church was sensitive to both—but especially so to those in the learning centers. In a remarkable series of conferences, seminary professors were sent out to the constituency as teachers of the church. Patiently and gracefully they accomplished the interpretive task, evoking new confidence from clergy and lay colleagues. While enhancing the best in scholarship, they expanded interpretations, but most certainly did not destroy the essentials of the faith. It was in this milieu that the church, with help from seminary people, produced a landmark teaching aid, *The Bible: Book of Faith.*

A Critical Distinction

How is this two-directional sensitivity relevant to current tensions as church and seminaries interact? Conversations in the marketplace indicate that there is considerable dissatisfaction with the use of words like *conservative* and *liberal.* The mood is such that for a significant number of Christians *conservative* conveys all that is good; *liberal* conveys all that is bad. The former suggests fidelity, devotion, defense of truth as it has been known. The latter—for them—suggests free and loose, betrayal, lack of integrity or concern.

These conclusions should be summarily rejected. They delimit both words. But it is the term *liberal* that I want to deal with here. The distinction I want to make is not between it and conservative, but between liberal theology and liberal scholarship. Liberal theology proceeds from certain presuppositions which are not palatable to Lutherans. Two are illustrative:

• Jesus was only a man like other men.

- What theologians need to do is to get behind the heterogeneity of all religious expression down to the psychological elements basic to all and there discover the unifying factors in acceptable common denominators.

Liberal theology thus defined is flatly rejected by our seminaries.

Liberal scholarship, on the other hand, uses all historical, etymological, and archeological tools to understand the thing as it is of itself. It does not attribute evil or maliciousness to the tools per se or methods per se.

It is very important that students of theology be able to handle distinctions and interpretive tools; yet, here is a dilemma. New perceptions cannot easily be infused into young people zealous for old securities, and a significant number of students entering seminaries today have certainly been influenced by literalist securities and motifs. Their devotion is single-eyed and earnest. A passion for simple answers, though, often closes the door to further study, and they settle too easily for "what works."

Such single-eyed devotion can become myopic tunnel vision; then confrontation becomes inevitable. Naive and zealous, they come face to face with professors who "blow their minds." These professors, disconcertingly, are Christ-confessing people; yet they use modern interpretive tools and methods and call into question the students' easy assumptions. "Is the professor a liar? a wolf in sheep's clothing? Are his interpretive challenges all right and are mine all wrong? Is my basic conviction about the Bible wrong? What am I to do? What am I to believe? What will I be able to preach and teach?"

Young men and women entering theological schools and seminaries, determined to "win the world for Christ," can—in this process—find themselves unstrung, overwhelmed by sophisticated teachers and new methods of study. Some never

57

come to grips with basic issues. They quit outright or fade away. Others revert to simplistic patterns of belief and develop schizoid approaches to theology and life. Some "resolve" the matter by foregoing both literal Bible reading and "liberal scholarship." They seek peace in a new spiritualism. This is one factor in the growth of Pentecostalism and pietism in the church.

Most struggle through. Childlike faith and venerable reason find confluence in a healthy adult synthesis. The struggle is necessary and two things generally happen: they see their faith in God and his Christ is not destroyed—may even be strengthened; and they find new confidence in having faced the honest questions of the world without subverting them. These people will be the church's best ministers, and they'll not be mediocre.

The Discreet Use of Truth

No seminary wishes to crush youthful idealism. No seminary wants as graduates cynics who work out personal frustrations at the expense of unsuspecting congregations. Truth is not put into a student's hands to be a destructive tool. Truth always has its counterpart, love. New-found knowledge must be accompanied by caring intent. I weary of fulminators who have to "dump it all on parishioners" making sure that they feel theologically inferior and morally second class. We have to start where people are. We may not like where they are, and properly will not want them to stay where they are, but where they are is the starting point.

I know of no better way of illustrating present churchly dilemmas and the need for sensitive truth-sharers than by using the classic introduction from Andrew Dickson White's classic, *A History of the Warfare of Science with Theology in Christendom.*

My book is ready for the printer, and as I begin this preface my eye lights upon the crowd of Russian peasants at work on the Neva under my windows. With pick and shovel they are letting the rays of the April sun into the great ice barrier which binds together the modern quays and the old granite fortress where lie the bones of the Romanoff Czars.

This barrier is already weakened; it is widely decayed, in many places thin, and everywhere treacherous; but it is, as a whole, so broad, so crystallized about old boulders, so imbedded in shallows, so wedged into crannies on either shore, that it is a great danger. The waters from thousands of swollen streamlets above are pressing behind it; wreckage and refuse are piling up against it; every one knows that it must yield. But there is danger that it may resist the pressure too long and break suddenly, wrenching even the granite quays from their foundations, bringing desolation to a vast population, and leaving, after the subsidence of the flood, a widespread residue of slime, a fertile breeding-bed for the germs of disease.

But the patient *mujiks* are doing the right thing. The barrier, exposed more and more to the warmth of spring by the scores of channels they are making, will break away gradually, and the river will flow on beneficent and beautiful.

My work in this book is like that of the Russian *mujik* on the Neva. I simply try to aid in letting the light of historical truth into that decaying mass of outworn thought which attaches the modern world to medieval conceptions of Christianity, and which still lingers among us—a most serious barrier to religion and morals and a menace to the whole normal evolution of society.

For behind this barrier also the flood is rapidly rising—the flood of increased knowledge and new thought; and this barrier also, though honeycombed and in many places thin, creates a danger —danger of a sudden breaking away, distressing and calamitous, sweeping before it not only outworn creeds and noxious dogmas, but cherished principles and ideals, and even wrenching out most precious religious and moral foundations of the whole social and political fabric.

My hope is to aid—even if it be but a little—in the gradual and healthful dissolving away of this mass of unreason, that the stream of "religion pure and undefiled" may flow on broad and clear, a blessing to humanity.

There are facets of Dr. White's enlightenment convictions and societal optimism that I most certainly disavow, but the example is dramatic, and there is truth in his analogy.

Theologically, this is our situation. We're frozen up by long winters of biblical credulity uninformed by conscientious reflection on what research has brought to light since the mid-nineteenth century. To "let the whole stream flow" will not only break the jam, it will destroy everything in its path; but to do nothing, to impede those necessary openings for truth, will only guarantee disaster.

Each pastor-preacher-teacher must be a "patient *mujik.*" He fails in his mission if he does not disassemble the great ice barrier. One who will not let the streamlets through is no friend. But if the pastor decides to tear down indiscriminately and psychotically wants truth to flow impeded by no other concern—then he may well destroy persons, congregations, and communities. Truth must be tempered by love. That's what seminaries are telling embryo clergy. Love cannot become an excuse for hiding from the truth. That's what seminaries are telling the church.

4 THE ROLE OF THE CONGREGATION

The ministry of the church to the world is truncated if it is exercised only as an individualistic thing. Lutherans at their best have consistently resisted a privatistic understanding of faith and privatistic forms of ministry. We realize that each Christian is to be a witness to Christ in this world, but we also have a genuine appreciation for the dominant congregational and corporate emphases marking the life of the apostolic church.

A few New Testament letters are addressed to single persons or are considered to have been written by single persons, but in citing those to Timothy, Titus, or Philemon, or the one by Jude, the inferences are still congregational. Major documents such as Romans, Corinthians, Galatians, and Ephesians are so patently rooted in ecclesiological motifs that they are not really understandable apart from those motifs. Even the writer of the Apocalypse gives support to the corporate dimension by spotlighting it in his letters to the seven churches of Asia Minor.

It is not necessary, however, to detail the history of congregational life from apostolic times to times atomic. Suffice it to say that most of us have come out of a corporate churchly background—a congregation and a denomination. We willingly share the confession of Cyprian, ". . . the church is our spiritual mother." But a mother's lot extends beyond that of bringing a fetus to birth and giving nurture to the young. Invariably there is maternal responsibility for arbitrating struggles, expressing love, sharing counsel, inspiring service, and fashioning a vision of the future. Ecclesiastically all these things are applicable to apostolic congregations—especially fashioning a vision for the future. The early church had a most vibrant sense of that future. Its members believed the end of history was already made known in Jesus Christ. They believed that the final realization of God's kingdom was at hand. The new aeon had come and they were part of it. Their very presence, they felt, was a sign to the world. Moreover, their source of power was not to be found in the traditions of a Jewish past, but in the personality of the Messiah Jew who enlivened their present and beckoned them to a new future.

Christ left his disciples with the promise that he would return. When this did not happen within their expected time span, hopes for the consummation of the kingdom dimmed. It was apocalypse later—not now! Moreover, the burst of ethical vitality linked so closely to eschatological hopes also tended to dissipate. Imperatives which seemed incontrovertible were weakened by doubt. But is there not a lesson here? Is it not axiomatic that if the church is to be a dynamic factor in life in any age it must maintain its eschatological hope and honor accordingly those imperatives which mark its unique mission in the world?

What imperatives were at work in apostolic congregations? Are they applicable for today? Four are worthy of review. The church was

1. to gather and distribute resources
2. to preach to, teach, and serve people regardless of station
3. to be an arena for dealing with conflict
4. to be a sign of the coming kingdom in the present world.

Imperative 1: *Gather and Distribute Resources*

Christian attitudes toward property and possessions emerged from Jesus' own testimony and from the fiery preaching of the apostles. Eric Hoffer says "change doesn't follow revolution, revolution follows change"—and the coming of Christ had changed everything. A "Christian revolution" followed, a revolution marked by dramatic shifts in dealing with one's acquisitive nature and one's attitude toward wealth. Striking changes may be seen in such New Testament passages as Luke 12 where Jesus tells his disciples not to be anxious because "life is more than food, and the body more than clothing;" and Acts 4:32-35 where the apostles shared their possessions "and distribution was made to each as any had need."

It is obvious that attitudes commonly sanctioned in society were considered base by Christians. The driving human passion to acquire was to be tamed. Christ's people were not to try to secure their existence in this world. They were to be characterized by new ways of thinking and a new way of living, and congregations were to be the corporate expression. They were to gather and distribute resources. This was a moral imperative. Even after Paul writes his most ethereal chapter on the resurrection, 1 Corinthians 15, his very next words are, "Now concerning the contribution for the saints. . . ."

What about our congregations? Well, the news isn't all bad and it isn't all good. We have our own Ananiases and Sapphiras but we have some marvellous unacclaimed saints as well. What we should measure, however, is not just the motivation and measure of individual generosity, but the motivation and measure of congregational generosity. On what are our resources expended? Are they gathered but then reserved for the congregation's own pleasure, satisfaction, and well being? Or is a significant portion of the total resource dis-

65

tributed for use elsewhere? We often chide social service agencies for having high administrative costs—how do ours run?

It is disconcerting when congregations become the objects of ministry rather than the subjects in ministering. All of us share that fault. As presently constituted most of our congregations are made up largely of white, middle-class persons victimized by and captive to class interests. Comparatively secure in our essential financial condition, rarely burning with social passion for people of other races and on different economic levels, we do just enough to qualify for inclusion in the non-profit category—but we are "non-prophet" as well.

No one exposed these contradictions in American Protestantism more penetratingly than Reinhold Niebuhr. In this moment when Europeans and Near-Easterners are talking about "selfish America" his words written in 1926 have an eerie, almost timeless quality:

The churches of America are on the whole thoroughly committed to the interests and prejudices of the middle classes. I think it is a bit of unwarranted optimism to expect them to make any serious contribution to the reorganization of society. I still have hopes that they will become sufficiently intelligent and heroic to develop some qualifying considerations in the great industrial struggle, but I can no longer envisage them as really determining factors in the struggle. Neither am I able for this reason to regard them as totally useless, as some of the critics do.

The middle classes are in fact quite incapable of any high degree of social imagination. Their experience is too limited to give them a clear picture of the real issues in modern industrial life. Non-union mines may organize in West Virginia and reduce miners to a starvation wage without challenging the conscience of a great middle class nation. If the children of strikers are starving it is more difficult to find support for them than to win contributors for the missions of the church. America may arouse the resentment of the world by its greed and all the good people of the American prairie will feel nothing but injured innocence from these European and Asiatic reactions to our greed. (*Leaves from the Notebooks of a Tamed Cynic,* p. 116.)

Lutherans are not "totally useless." They have written great pages in "the book of generosity"—Lutheran World Action, Lutheran World Relief, The Hunger Appeal, Bread for the World. Yet, these are basically relief measures. They do not affect the essential economic structures in the ordering of society. Do Christians and Christian churches not have a larger role to play? Yes, we gather and distribute resources for remedial aid, but how or when do we deal with the amazing economic power of the West, challenge the multi-national corporations, assess the great inequities in American culture and world culture, and seek ways in which we can both alleviate poverty and enhance prosperity? How can we handle it so that it is not just beneficial for the privileged few, but for the underprivileged many? Class interests must be challenged and social imagination must be awakened. Congregations should look at what isn't being done on 43rd and Halsted in Chicago, or Hastings Street in Detroit, before complimenting themselves unduly for contributions given to missions in Africa. Read the pathos of this fine Black leader and ask whether remedial measures are enough:

After 12 years of party activism, Earl Craig Jr. has given up his fight to make the Democratic Party more responsive to the problems of the poor.

The problem, Craig said, was not with his enemies in the party's conservative wing, but with his so-called friends and allies in the liberal establishment.

"My greatest frustration was that the people I'm closest to, which is the liberal wing, are often the ones I have the most difficulty making understand the issues of income redistribution," Craig said.

The trouble with liberals, "the so-called good people," as Craig puts it, is that "the things that . . . are truly important to them are not poor and working people. They don't want anything harmful to happen to them. They would like to see them do better. But in their gut their concerns are not the concerns of the bottom third of our society." (*The Minneapolis Star*, Monday, Jan. 7, 1980.)

Imperative 2: *Preach, Teach, Serve*

Hand in glove with the gathering and distribution of resources is the imperative to preach to, teach, and serve people regardless of station. Visser 't Hooft wrote,

Many reasons could be given for the sickness of our parishes, but the chief of all reasons is their failure to recognize the living authority of the Word which has made them and which alone can remake them. If the Word is to become alive two things are necessary: a truly biblical preaching which is not only addressed to all but is shared by all, and a common effort in Bible study. (Op. cit. p. 36).

Preaching and teaching are priority items. They dare never be minimized. When current evaluations are made of difficult places where pastors and congregations are really "making it," we find a not so surprising fact—they are working at proclamation, teaching, worshiping, and serving. Volumes . have been written on preaching and teaching but it is the "orphan element"—*service* which merits expanded consideration.

According to the Bible, the Christian life is service or ministry. For the Christian is the disciple of Him who came not to be served but to serve (Mark x. 45). Ministry does not consist only in bearing witness but in the act of charity to a neighbour (Matt. xxv.). And it is carried out not only on behalf of the members of the Church family, but for all the others for whom Christ died. The Christian is "the servant of *all*" (Mk. ix. 35).
So the ministry of the Christian is neither restricted to the Church, nor detached from it. (Ibid. p. 43).

This "orphan element", *diakonia* or service, has had such a tortuous history. Arthur Seegers observes that "Emperor Constantine . . . made the effective charitable endeavors to be something like a welfare department of his empire. . . . physical properties were put into the control of the bishops." However, just as the "sacrificial" and the "teaching" functions in Israel suffered dichotomy, so did the "service" and the "preaching-teaching-sacrament giving" elements in pre-Reformation Catholicism. Seegers continues, "The Reformers . . . set their minds to putting diakonia as service to the poor into the mind and practice of the congregation again. They achieved little more than a mindset. . . ."

The Reformers put emphasis on preaching the Word. The deacon was not needed for this, nor was he needed at the celebration of the Lord's Supper. Preachers easily achieved monopoly of the congregation as audience for them. . . .
This model of the sermon-hearing congregation was transplanted to America and is currently maintained here. (Seegers, Unpublished lecture, Jan. 1974).

The state churches gravitated inexorably to essential "religious" activities such as preaching, teaching, and worshiping. The state assumed responsibility for handling the "service needs" of the citizens. Each drew its area of activity around its gravitational pole. Thus the bifurcation between worship-learning and service elements became more and more severe.
It wasn't until the mid-nineteenth century that radical *diakonal* concerns were brought again to the fore. Marx did it first of all in a most indicting revolutionary fashion. His fundamental proposition, described by Friedrich Engels in

The Communist Manifesto was this,
. . . that in every historical epoch, the prevailing mode of economic production and exchange, and the social organization necessarily following from it, form the basis on which is built up . . . the political and intellectual history of that epoch; that consequently the whole history of mankind has been a history of class struggles . . . exploiting and exploited, ruling and oppressed . . . that . . . a stage has been reached where the exploited and oppressed class, the proletartiat, cannot attain its emancipation . . . without at the same time . . . emancipating society at large from all exploitation, oppression, class distinction, and class struggles. . . . the proletarians have nothing to lose but their chains. They have a world to win. Workingmen of all countries, unite!

He saw the way in which the church had identified itself with those in power; and despairing of any change in the church or in the ruling class, he became the adversary of both.

In the same year that the *Manifesto* was published, 1848, another man had something to say about service. His name was Johann Hinrich Wichern. Here was a churchman who 15 years earlier started out on a systematically planned work among young people in the slums of Hamburg. Wichern felt it was the business of the church to seek out precisely those groups excluded by the privileged facets of society, and neglected by it, in order to save the lost. This was deliberate "salvation by identification." He felt we must stand with the poor of the earth. Redemption had to be a social as well as a theological reality. He raised anew the significance of the relationship between the Word proclaimed and works of charity and, therefore, the diaconal element in the life of the church. Laymen were regarded as servants of the church, persons not burdened with pastoral duties, persons identified as brothers.

This revivification of *diakonia* is critical for present Lutheranism and all of Christendom. If there is anyone in ALC ranks to thank for its resurrection, it is that grand gentleman, the aforementioned Reverend Arthur J. Seegers. He has been our voice in the wilderness of diaconal neglect. His official service climaxed aiding, directing, abetting social service agencies whose origin was usually outside of the formal congregational structures. Such agencies were often the creation of one caring spirit, or maybe a few—now they seek better and more intimate relationships with the organized church. Church and agencies have been deprived because of the lack of the other's involvement. They are part of the current challenge but additional things must be emphasized at this point, things having to do with the more radical and cosmic dimensions of *diakonia*.

It is not appropriate, as has been said, to limit the church's social concern to remedial categories. Lutherans must help to inspire new structures, or at least new attitudes in old structures for enhancing the well-being of the poor and disenfranchized. Work can be done on an individual basis but the real clout comes when congregations and the church at large face up to corporate ethical challenges.

A rather spirited debate arises when we face the question "how do congregations implement such diaconal concern?" One view says, "re-establish the office of deacon. In so doing you make visible the broader concern and people have a weekly reminder that service is just as much a part of church life as preaching and teaching." But this has its limitations. By establishing a single office we can relieve corporate conscience and end up isolating the very factor we wish to broaden. Furthermore, some have already created a guild of liturgical deacons consisting of those few who have a modicum of ritual expertise. This doesn't touch the problems we have been talking about. Yet still others would borrow the diaconal concepts and content of Roman Catholicism and Anglicanism. The net effect can be nothing radically different than what inheres in the liturgical deacon and is really a first step into an official priesthood.

Lutherans have not generally found these options very palatable—at least not American Lutherans. Our ideas might better approximate Luther's, "let us have those who distribute goods, care for the sick, and see who is suffering need." Add Wichern's concern for "those groups excluded by the privileged facets of society and neglected by it." Add still further an exacerbated need "to redress inequities and dare to revamp structures for a more equitable distribution of resources." This, and nothing less, is the scope of *diakonia*. We must raise every congregation's consciousness to this level. What must be enhanced is not a clerical collar mentality but a blue collar mentality—with sleeves rolled up. The hardest question is not "what offices should the church have?" but "how can we marshal the power of the church to serve the world?"

If we do not isolate the office of deacon what do we do? I say use those existing structures which are already a part of each congregation's life, specifically the church council. But do not approach the matter having suspended your critical faculties. In the *Model Constitution and Bylaws for Congregations of the American Lutheran Church* we have these two references to deacons:

Designate _____ of its members, including the president, to serve as the Board of Deacons of the congregation. This board shall provide spiritual leadership in the congregation, working with the pastor, to guide the work, witness, worship, and service of the congregation in the world. The pastor shall be an advisory member of the Board of Deacons by virtue of office but without vote. (p. 7).

Duties and Responsibilities of the Board of Deacons

In addition to the duties and responsibilities provided in the constitution, the Board of Deacons shall:

1. Elect from its own membership a chairman and a secretary.

2. Conduct regular meetings not less than once each month at such time and place as the board may determine.

3. Develop a program of evangelism.

4. Consider matters relating to the worship of the congregation, and make recommendations to the annual meeting.

5. Initiate and implement witness and service in the community. (p. 18).

The key phrases for understanding what a deacon is *are last* in each section—"service of the congregation in the world," and "service in the community." Most never get to that. They get hung up on liturgical items and that being the case, how do you ever get them out of the altar guild?

Put *diakonia* in first place. It is a travesty to let deacons be preoccupied with administrative affairs, much less give prime time and energy to ushering, and chancel care. Let them have major responsibility in assessing the needs of people the church should be serving and let them be the catalysts in marshaling congregational support and involvement. Our great challenge is how to make congregations true diaconal units. Redefinition of terms and duties must serve that end.

Imperative 3: *Dealing with Conflict*

What justification is there for talking about the church as an arena for dealing with conflict? More than most of us think! In dealing with *ministry, The Lutheran Encyclopedia* indicates

> . . . that the early church also had an assembly of the many to settle disputes and matters of administration which concerned the whole church (Acts 6:2, 15:12). This was no democratic society with a balance of interests protected by pressure groups and elected representatives. Nor was there the fiction of a transfer of function from the many to a few who then served on behalf of the many to keep order. The structure is rather that of an *organic unity* which existed in spite of inequalities but lived in freedom as the various members of a healthy body live and work together. In cases of difference of opinion the opposition was always expected to concur out of loyalty to the whole. This whole structure must be understood as it was animated by the living presence of the Word and Spirit. (Vol. II, pp. 1580-1581).

For many the introduction, or even the acknowledgement of conflicting opinions in the life of a congregation is something to avoid like the plague. Peace, oneness of mind, these are the preferred states. It has taken us an unbelievably long time to see that raising both sides of a moral issue is not necessarily a sign of disintegration or unhealth—it is to the contrary a sign of maturity and vitality. To thus engage the church is not to threaten it or destroy it, it is one of the best ways of keeping the church alive and credible.

Look at two illustrations, one ancient, one modern. The

former deals with a major personality conflict between the two greatest leaders of the apostolic period, Peter and Paul. A basic principle was at stake and Paul airs the issue with brutal honesty in his letter to the Galatians. His candor is without reserve.

> But when Cephas came to Antioch I opposed him to his face, because he stood condemned. For before certain men came from James, he ate with the Gentiles; but when they came he drew back and separated himself, fearing the circumcision party. And with him the rest of the Jews acted insincerely, so that even Barnabas was carried away by their insincerity. But when I saw that they were not straightforward about the truth of the gospel, I said to Cephas before them all, "If you, though a Jew live like a Gentile and not like a Jew, how can you compel the Gentiles to live like Jews?" (Gal. 2:11-14).

The matter of Gentile inclusion was one of the earliest points of tension in the Christian community. Would they have to submit to Jewish ordinances before becoming Christians, or not? Peter's failure to uphold the apostolic decision not to make circumcision a requisite to table fellowship was overcome by Paul's stout stance. What should be underscored is that the controversy was dealt with in the church's context and resolved in that context.

Controversy and conflict are also present realities, things we must deal with. The late 1960s were marked by strife and tension. Consistent with past history, Lutherans regarded the state as "the left hand of God." Now they were impaled on the horns of a dilemma. The government was pursuing a war adventure in Viet Nam and their own children, sons and daughters of an affluent generation, were venting displeasure with wide spread adult hypocrisy, and unconcern about the war. Washington was guilty of deceit and aggression. Educational institutions were bereft of integrity. Churches preached social concern but perpetuated class interest and racial prejudice. Wealthy parents gave lip service to Christian ideals but their lives were vapid and contradictory. Young idealists stormed and raged, burned draft cards, defied the state, fled the country.

The church's initial response was not a distinguished one. A tradition of compliance to government and uncritical attitudes toward its leaders were psychological chains not easily cast off. Never had there been a time of nonconformity in American Lutheran Church life like this one. Could hawks and doves meet anywhere? What organization could tolerate such strident differences? Was there any membrane that could take the strain? Did a power exist which could serve a cohesive purpose without violating perceived integrity on either side? Answer—the congregation! The Christian congregation! The love of Christ in the Christian congregation!

Lamentably some congregations then and some congregations now seek to avoid the truly grievous but critical questions of life. They even protract them by deciding nothing. Thus credibility evaporates and despair "creeps in on big cat feet." But why such stress on the Christian congregation? Why such passion for this context? Because it is the best membrane, maybe the only membrane or cell, which trustees a power able to ameliorate the worst of relationships. A ready analogy is at hand in this model from the biological world. In his book *Lives of a Cell*, Dr. Lewis Thomas writes,

It takes a membrane to make sense out of disorder in biology. You have to be able to catch energy and hold it, storing precisely the needed amount and releasing it in measured shares. A cell does this, and so do the organelles inside. Each assemblage is poised in the flow of solar energy, tapping off energy from metabolic surrogates of the sun. To stay alive, you have to be able to hold out against equilibrium, maintain inbalance, bank against entropy, and you can only transact this business with membranes in our kind of world. (p. 170f.).

Within the membrane of the congregation we "hold out against equilibrium, maintain imbalance, bank against entropy." Only here can we take competing agents, mutually repellent particles, and have them interact without destroying each other. The energy which sustains this "cell" is not solar energy, but the Son's gift of love. Love is the power which holds Christians together—chiefly God's love for us, only reflectively our love for each other—and Christians are the cohesive force which helps hold the world together. Perhaps nothing is more wearing and grievous than dealing with conflict, but the churches in general and the congregations in particular contradict human reality when they act as though conflict doesn't exist—or when they beg the issue by retreating into a supposed spirituality.

Imperative 4: *A Sign of the Kingdom*

In his Sermon on the Mount our Lord uses the figure of light to underscore the character of the Christian presence in the world.

You are the light of the world. A city set on a hill cannot be hid. Nor do men light a lamp and put it under a bushel . . . . Let your light so shine before men, that they may see your good works and give glory to your Father who is in heaven (Matt. 5:14-16)

The church is God's light, his sign, in this world of darkness. But what does the sign mean, what does it point to? Only the most dramatic of facts—this old aeon dominated by sin and death has had its power broken! A new aeon has come. Jesus Christ is himself a sign of that kingdom even as his people are a sign of that kingdom. Thus he can say "I am the light of the world . . . you are the light of the world." The consummation of the kingdom lies in the future but the sign is here.

Analogically we might turn the comparison to the American hostages in Iran. They languish under the power of those who hold them in bondage and darkness. They are a symbol of the world under the old aeon. What do they long for? Is it not release, freedom, a new future, a sign that this might be? Accordingly small groups of visitors have come. They represent the world beyond Teheran, the possibility of a future. They are a "sign." They point to a reality beyond themselves. They are not the reality, they only represent it.

The imprisoned can live in light of that sign and hope, or in the darkness in which they are held. They can say "we will hope and trust in that new future," or they can say "O yes—you talk about freedom and the overcoming of captivity, but look at these garrisons in which we are held! See these bands on our wrists, the blindfolds on our eyes!"

People in our world feel like that, even some in the church. Present despair tends to overwhelm future hope. But the truth stands. Darkness has not overcome the light. Even though evil rages the future is God's, and the church is his sign of that future.

Unbelief is hard to kill. The old aeon does not willingly pass away. Is there some basic reason for the hostility between the world and the church? What is it that the world hates and fears? What does "the light" disclose and reveal? Karl Barth puts his finger on the crux of the matter:

The world's secret is the non-existence of its gods. At the price of floods of tears and blood, the world keeps denying its secret and seeks to populate nature and history with its idols. The deep reason of its unrest is its refusal to confess its profane character. The Church is aware of this secret of the world. It must not permit itself to be befuddled by reproaches and accusations. Just so it is truly loyal to the world.
But this faithfulness of the Church to the world is after all possible only as the reverse side of an entirely different loyalty. The Church is in existence where man hears God. Not gods, not something divine, but God. (*God in Action*, p. 28)

So, the church is a sign of this peoples *yes* to God and *no* to the world—but their *no* to the world is their ultimate way of affirming the world because the world is God's. The church is a sign of that future reign which will be evident to all, but it is also a sign that the kingdom is a present reality, denied by many. Only when the church has the most vibrant sense of the future can it bring hope to those who languish in the present. Only when it is true to *the light* can it be a light in the darkness.

5 CONGREGATIONAL CONSCIENCE AND COMMUNITY CONCERN

In 1948 Harper and Brothers published a book entitled *The Plight of Freedom*. The author was the eminent Lutheran pastor, Paul Scherer. The basic axiom was that freedom "rests not on any democratic theory of tolerance, not on any social legislation, not on the rights of the individual . . . but on the spiritual stature of mankind" (p. 1). Dr. Scherer saw this stature in jeopardy. This was traceable, in part, to the erosion of conscience. He said, "I am not worried about the dawn of conscience. I am worried about its twilight. Not who had it first, but who had it last. Not where on earth it came from, but where on earth, in very plain speech, it has gone" (p. 94).

In most instances our discussions of conscience have centered on individuals—too much so. We have neglected the corporate dimensions. Of all institutions the church must be the very first to repent of this wrong precisely because its mandate has to do with "the spiritual stature of mankind." Just as evil is not only individual but collective and corporate in nature, and must be dealt with that way, so too for conscience. What, we now must ask, is the state of the collective conscience of the church?

The benchmark followed in this assessment is how conscience is constrained to work, or not work, in its concern for community. But a statement on the limitations of congregational polity must precede the assessment. Three points of vulnerability stand out:

1. Congregationalism can assimilate the spirit of individualism in such a way that the individualism of the person becomes the individualism of the congregation.
2. In spite of the polity aim that congregations should affiliate with those of like mind, the corporate intention and amalgamation tends to be more theory than practice.
3. Seldom can congregations, by themselves, influence structures and address the needs of society in the most effective way.

This is not a campaign against congregationalism. That is, after all, an essential element in our polity, but since it has such common application in Lutheran circles, we must question its viability for corporate social action. Who will deny that the time has come for us to do more effectively on district and national levels what a few socially concerned congregations have been trying to do locally?

Agony and Ecstasy—Our Church's Social Consciousness

The last quarter of a century gives Lutherans no immediate cause for rejoicing. Work in urban areas, considered such a potential strength before World War II, is now deemed by many a liability. Interim salvage efforts were attempted. The National Lutheran Council, predecessor body of The Lutheran Council—U.S.A., made gallant attempts to energize and redirect church work in the great metropolitan centers. Self studies were conducted. Congregational profiles were developed—and the implications were ominous. To the extent that congregations were not serving people in their immediate context, to the extent that leadership was moving away from the concentric heart, they were in the process of disintegration. Most lamentable of all, decisions of what to do and how to do it were left with the local units. With shrinking constituency and diminished life the alternatives seemed narrowed to one—move! Academicians, now two decades removed, sagely comment "this rush to the suburbs in the 1950s and 1960s is the root of our present problems." We must demur. That exodus wasn't nearly as much a cause as it was a result. It was a clear manifestation of the fact that the church had not taken the great metropolitan centers seriously. Is there any doubt? Examine this choice bit of history.

Dr. E. W. Mueller, speaking to the Chicago Mission Society, cited a precise area "that was and is in need of the mission concern of the church." The year, 1954. He described an area bounded by Chicago Avenue on the north, 47th Street on the south, Lake Michigan on the east, and Cicero Avenue on the west. His analysis, "this area has more than one million inhabitants. Some parts of the area are declining in population, others are increasing quite rapidly. The overall population of the area is on the increase. There was a time when the Lutheran church had quite a few congregations here, (perhaps 33-35) but today, 1954, there are only seven National Lutheran Council congregations and eighteen Lutheran Church-Missouri Synod congregations—a total of twenty-five congregations for more than one million people."

He used a comparison to dramatize the mission responsibility of the National Lutheran Council congregations in this area—"the combined population of North Dakota and South Dakota is a little more than one million three hundred thousand persons. This is about the same number of people living in the area described above. In the Chicago area we have seven National Lutheran Council congregations, in the Dakota areas we have more than five hundred congregations! The ratio, 71-1. "The heart of Chicago presents the Lutherans with a real mission assignment," he concluded. The antecedent bodies of the present American Lutheran Church had *one* congregation in that area.

The fact that other ethnic groups were not sought out as

desirable partners underscores the judgment that both the leaders and the led had little heart for urban realities. The consequence? Lutherans lived with a condemning rather than a commanding conscience. This was true on a national level, a district level, and on the congregational level. Only a very few reached out. No strategy developed, no monetary resource pool was accumulated, no moral and prophetic leadership was given to congregations. The noose of self interest tightened. Ministry came to mean ministry to members. Lost was the sense of being priests for others. Vanished, the image of the church as a priesthood serving the world. Convert racism could not go unnoticed.

Dark faces and almond eyes were not considered an appropriate part of the scene. One by one Lutheran congregations withered, and many died. The autopsies had a monotonous sameness; lack of evangelical fervor and social concern, movement of leadership away from the geographic center, apathy toward new ethnic neighbors, lack of planning among corporate leaders, meager support from other congregations, inability to work in cross-cultural settings. And what was true for Chicago was true for all the great cities. It was what Paul Scherer called "the twilight of conscience."

Two hundred and seventy miles east lies Detroit. Were the processes and effects in Chicago unique or were they in fact the same for all cities, including the Motor City? Here is a response from Dr. Reginald Holle, president of the Michigan District of the American Lutheran Church. "From 1970 to 1978 the baptized membership of our congregations in the Detroit area has dropped from 41,000 to 28,000, a loss of 31%. If that rate of decline is maintained over the next twenty years, the American Lutheran Church in this part of the country will be out of existence." Dr. Holle believes in the strategy "Forward to Basics." He considers this the antidote for present trends. Moreover, "we may have gone through an era of clergy dominance and relatively low regard for lay membership, but the '80s are urging us to be confessionally and scripturally aware of our distinct, yet mutual, function in the body of believers."

What is described is a denial of catholicity, not just theological, but sociological. The problem goes beyond race prejudice, it was and is a matter of class prejudice and class interest as well. Many clergy readily identify with Kiwanis, Rotary, Lions, Optimists—but how many identify with labor unions? Maybe that too is passé, maybe this day calls for still different affiliations. But how genuine is our social consciousness?

———————

Lest anyone be left with the illusion that it is only the urban conscience which has faltered, move over to Wisconsin, Minnesota, the Dakotas, and the mountain States. Did rural congregations address the wider community more effectively? Was conscience clean when removed from smog? Sin doesn't start at the city limits and it doesn't end there. We have, for example, three hundred congregations adjacent to or in the vicinity of large segments of the Native American population. The paucity of their numbers in our midst is testimony enough that the mindset and the heartbeat of Lutherans in rural areas is much akin to that in urban areas.

Priests for others? the whole church a priestly community for the world? Agony, brothers and sisters, agony! Conscience may have gone, for a season, but now it returns to haunt us.

Someone is sure to say "Well, Indians and Blacks and Hispanics are not really interested in us. Your so-called wider community doesn't care if we are there or not. They could have come to us, you know!" Some did. At least some tried. No, if these groups suffer alienation, the fault is mainly ours. We have not been obedient to our own evangelical mandates.

We have been conscienceless. We think we know what is going on in others, but we really don't. It's like Father Rank's observation in Graham Greene's *The Heart of the Matter:*

The Church knows all the rules. But it doesn't know what goes on in a single human heart (p. 306).

Churches have to proceed out of their own self-understanding and loyalty to the gospel, but they must also proceed with an understanding of context and the people in it. We must be sensitive to their deep longings whether they are believing or unbelieving. The community may even see reasons for the churches existence which the church doesn't see, so let's suspend, for the moment, our witness to the community, and let the community have its say to the church!

The Community's Witness to the Church

The name of Studs Terkel doesn't appear in many theological school bibliographies. Lawyer turned newspaperman, radio personality, author, he is the champion of the common people, some of whose interviews come from the very areas we have alluded to. How does this testimony from *Division Street: America* challenge our corporate conscience?

Florence Scala, 47—product of Hull House:
You know, there's a real kind of ugliness among nice people. You know, the dirty stuff that you think only hoodlums pull off. They can really destroy you, the nice people.
Sometimes I want to defend the rotten politicians in my neighborhood. I sometimes want to defend even gangsters. They don't pretend to be anything but what they are. You can see what they are. They're not fooling anybody, see? But nice people fool you (p. 32).

Stan Lenard, 45—actor and homosexual:
I was away from the church for two years, and I learned more about myself and my problems and the world than in thirty-five years of going to confession. The church always made me feel

like I was better than anybody else because I was a Catholic. One day I realized: How can anyone feel they are better than anyone else and still be part of the world, able to give and take. I think this is why things are changing so drastically in the church.

I don't feel guilty any more, but I feel being a homosexual is wrong. It's wrong because of the upheaval it creates within a person.

An innocence, that's what's lacking in so many supposedly adult human beings today. So many people are ashamed to cry, ashamed to really have feelings. I must include myself in this group, because maybe this is the reason I have not been able to open myself up to accept anyone else in my life. You meet so few people who do have the capacity for it (pp. 76-77).

Sister Evelyn, 26—Roman Catholic nun:
Any person who attempts to shake an institution has to be willing to take the consequences. We certainly don't look upon ourselves as prophets. We look upon ourselves as people who are testing a situation. But in the testing, we have to infringe on certain notions that have become traditionally accepted.

A Christian must be involved in sustained human relationships, because this is where Christ is found (pp. 143, 147).

Jimmy White 18—Black youth
I really don't want all that much out of the world. I don't figure the world owe me nothin' at all. If anything, I owe the world somethin' (p. 395).

Lily Lowell, 16—White youth
Most of the kids around here, who do they have to identify with? Every child is supposed to identify with something or someone. Or they try to identify with so many people that they get confused.

What are they looking for?
Security. Reassurance that life may get better. That they can make something of themselves. Confidence, they need someone to push it up just a little bit. And they just don't get it (p. 399).

Jessie Binford, 90—Hull House resident
When you look to the older people for what the young should find in them, it isn't there. Nothing's there. Do we have to wait for these young people to grow up and awaken those who are older? (p. 407).

These are the voices of the *hoi poloi,* the citizens. There is a mordant quality in them, disappointment, frustration, yet hope. It makes one think of another statement, "The whole creation groans in travail, awaiting the manifestation of the sons of God." But let's move off the streets and into city hall. Do municipal officials have a mean estimate of churches? What do they think about the importance of congregations for communities? Consider these:

Richard J. Daley, Chicago (deceased)
This mayor freely witnessed to the importance of churches for community life. His "Back-of-the-Yards Council" always had clergy involvement. He saw congregations as stabilizing and unifying forces. "The churches are the most important part of Chicago's life. We need leaders for our youth. Without you pastors and priests we lose a generation of good citizens."

Mike Royko writes of Daley, "Since childhood he . . . attended daily Mass. . . . On Sundays and some workdays he'll go to his own church. . . . Regardless of what he may do in the afternoon, or to whom, he will always pray in the morning." . . . "The Nativity Church was the center of the community. . . . The Church and the local political office provided most of the social welfare benefits." (*Boss,* pp. 13, 33-34).

Frank P. Zeidler, Milwaukee
In a Continuing Forum on Church and Society in 1970, Mr. Zeidler did a review of the world situation which he and his audience both regarded as pessimistic. Moving toward his conclusion he asked, "In the face of this, what might organized religion do about the amelioration of the coming conditions?" He had nineteen suggestions—it is sufficient to identify these six:

1. The Church should call for arms limitations, and the U.S.A. should quit supplying dictators the world over with armaments.
2. The Church should speak against a new isolationism, but should support U.S. efforts to raise the standards of developing countries.
3. The Church should earnestly work on the theological aspects

of the new world order, including the presence of weapons capable of destroying enormous masses of humanity.

4. The Church should spend much more effort on sorting out for youth what life styles lead to freedom and what lead to degradation and death.

5. The Church should reflect more on what constitutes a just economic order.

6. The Church shoul dseek to understand the forces of ethnic separatism and formulate an ethical set of principles about that phenomenon.

He concluded by saying, "Religious bodies must think through their theology in terms of new knowledge. If a man believes he is redeemed by God from eternal death, how does he translate this into everyday living? What should be his attitude toward the society around him? I do not think enough of this has been done effectively, and this in itself is a major goal of religion today, because religious beliefs express themselves in government actions very quickly." (*Published Speech,* Lutheran School of Theology, Chicago, Ill., January 8, 1970.)

Al Hofstede, Minneapolis
"I'm one of those politicians who believes that the churches (i.e. communities of faith, including synagogues) set the standard for life in society. We can pass all the laws in the world but finally we cannot coerce obedience. Nor can we create real conscience by coercive means. The impetus must come from our pulpits. Ministers and laity together have to show where trust is and by that means enhance the quality of community life. When that fails it's all gone. I've seen it in community after community.
The Church is people . . . we must find out what the Bible says and we must put into practice what we've been taught. People are searching everywhere for peace of mind. The church should realize what it is and live up to its own standards. Love has application in the immediate context. You have to love where you are. God isn't going to judge us only by what we did, but by what we didn't do. Churches do not have a diminished or passive role. They have a most influential role if they'll only exercise it. We cannot rebuild American cities, i.e. communities unless we have the impetus coming from the church, setting standards and teaching us how we should live together." (Quote, March 13, 1980)

These officials are unanimous in endorsement of religious institutions. Churches are not simply places of refuge or moral forces, they are signs of hope. Perhaps our reasons for maintaining their presence in community life are not identical with those of city officials or the citizens cited, but they are not exclusionary and we must learn to be sensitive listeners and better neighbors. A congregation, or a church body, without a community conscience will end up serving only itself. But not everything is agony. There is more than gloom and doom. The conscience of the church is not dead, there are flashes of ecstasy! Signs are increasing that the Lord of the church has touched consciences and urges us to embrace moral imperatives in unprecedented modern ways. People can be cynical about that and tell us it's all too little too late. Yet, better something than nothing. And who can predict the cumulative effect of caring acts done in good conscience? Let's share a few:

Investment in Black-owned Banks

In 1968 The American Lutheran Church invested a maximum amount of insured deposit in twenty banks owned by Blacks across America. In actual dollar amount the total was not that significant. What was significant was the declaration in their behalf and the entree it gave these banks in working with a much larger constituency. This action was a step beyond remedial action, it was an action which could help change present economic structures.

A similar effort was made in behalf of the M-REIT Program, Mutual Real Estate Investment Fund. Black owned housing development companies had the benefit of church support.

Ordinance 174

In a midwestern city a civil rights amendment came before the governing council of the municipality. It was on the agenda because a socially conscious and concerned congregation had struggled with others to get it there. Ordinance 174 suffered an initial 3-2 defeat, but it eventually became the rallying point for a "rights amendment" which passed.

A Face-to-face Ministry

From accusing conscience to commanding conscience is the story of Lutherans response to the plight of South Asian refugees. Mrs. Tinka Bloedow reports—"From 1975 through 1979, 34,235 refugees were sponsored by all Lutheran bodies; 33,591 were Indochinese, 438 were Latin American, 149 were Kurds, 57 were from other countries (Ethiopia etc.). In 1979 The American Lutheran Church had 824 sponsorships, (that is probably around 2,500 people). . . . The goal for Lutheran churches is to maintain about 500 sponsorships per month. About 5,000 Lutheran congregations have been involved in this total venture."

Christian Service Center—Orlando, Florida

"In the early 1970s, some Christian congregations, their pastors, and a few judicatories relating to the Orlando area were motivated by their faith to want to address the needs of their community through Christian service. They established the Christian Service Center. . . . From the very beginning the leadership has come from the laity with the pastors being the enablers, and the congregations and their individual members providing the basic financial support. . . . Throughout the years one need has stood out, *hunger.* . . . Seven days a week, the . . . Center feeds from 200-300 persons. . . . Three of the five services are mobilized to attack hunger. . . . Their Meals on Wheels program has an additional 500 daily recipients, and there are close to 1000 volunteers from the churches doing what the 30 volunteers did initially." The service transcends barriers of economics, age, race, and denominational difference. Catholic and Protestant from almost 150 churches affiliated with 22 different denominations work side by side to help those in need. (Information from Rev. William J. Kiether, March 15, 1980.)

Nothing awakens conscience like obedience to God's Word, and nothing reverses crippling centripetal forces quite like the commitment "to be a priest for others." The beautiful part of all these endeavors is that the principle guiding them was and is "no strings attached."

Conscience and Courage . .

In 1976 the Religious News Service had a headline, "Church's Honesty, Dependability Greater Than Its 'Ability to Get Things Done'." (Oct. 19, 1976). In January of 1980 the same Service had another headline, "Report Calls 'Clear Structure' Key to Successful Parish Work." The first was a general affirmation of integrity with some doubt about efficiency, the second, dealing with the Roman Catholic Church, posits ineffectiveness in poor structures. There is no doubt that structures are important, and that what is said of Catholics can just as well be said of others, but inability and malaise are traceable to something far more fundamental than structure—viz., a failure of nerve. That, most generally, is the product of an amoral conscience. Conversely, is not moral courage the quality which characterizes the most effective leaders in Christendom? Statesmanship, faith, intellectual brilliance, self-effacing love all have their place, but they are only conversation pieces without moral courage. Martin Luther King is a marvelous case in point. He had peers in many areas of life, he was not an original theologian, he borrowed much of his rhetoric, but the thing that set him apart was his tenacity to espouse and lead people in an unpopular but righteous cause. Moral courage made him fearless, and feared.

But is it even right to extol this quality when the foremost Greek word for courage, *andreia*, doesn't appear in the New Testament? (*Tharseo*, a much softer word, often translated *courage*, does appear.) Scholars debate its absence, some saying it is due to an ancient identifiability with war and military heroism, others saying it is excluded because it implies too much self-reliance and not enough dependence on God. However, a particular word is not as important as the reality and, who will doubt that our biblical heroes were courageous in the deepest sense of the word? Vis-a-vis the thesis intimating that courage originates in the self and the self's freedom from God, we have to remember what was true in their sequence of relationships. Courage was related to conscience and conscience was most surely rooted in God!

So Joseph rejects the opportunity to escape prison and he rebukes Potiphar's wife by saying, "how can I do this great wickedness and sin against God?" He, God, was, is, and shall be, the source of all principled activity.

At the root of all that God does is love. God not only loves, he is love, and he acts consistently with that which is his *esse* and marks his being. When the Lord Christ hangs on the cross this is not the act of a Stoic, resigned to fate, it is the conscience-driven deed of a God who will give himself in love and who will settle for nothing less than reconciliation with his creatures. Once Christians are captured by that love how can they remain the captives of structure? They re-fashion structure! The question can no longer be "What is expedient?" but "What is right?" Self, survival, or structure cannot be paramount, one thing is paramount, principled activity emerging from a good conscience and a courageous and loving heart.

Each of us must ask, "Am I willing to act courageously out of a good conscience rooted in God?" The response must not only be individual it must be collective, for we are members together in the Body of Christ. We know too well that we have been affected by culture far more than we have affected culture. We are clergy who have succumbed to the Chamber of Commerce mentality. We are laity molded by Madison Avenue. We all wait for leadership which is conscience driven, courageous, principled and worthy of the name—but we do not think often enough of being that leadership. We pray for bishops and theological students and pastors and lay partners and church officials who are bold and willing to live faithful to God and faithful to the world. Can we pass our time thinking God will answer by sending someone else? Community concerns will mean nothing to our congregations and our church unless we have the temerity to address them. Courage will be fleeting if we do not have a commanding conscience. Conscience, to be commanding, has to take God and his love seriously. . . .Marx thought the most revolutionary force in the world was a proletariat which had thrown off its chains. I believe the most revolutionary force in the world is a church whose conscience has been nailed to the cross.

6 THE CONGREGATION VIS-A-VIS THE DENOMINATION

At the heart of our church's life is a structural paradox which is both satisfying and exasperating. One part of it accents the autonomy of the local congregation. The other part accents the wider ecclesiastical authority of districts, synods, and the national church. Lutheran Christians should be able to relate well to both entities, and many do, but some congregations, and a smattering of members in other congregations, simply do not keep the two loyalties in balance. Local units are understandably independent, eager to regulate their own life and determine their own destiny. District units and national offices, however, symbolize compulsion to conformity for the sake of a greater collective effectiveness. The tension between them is the classic tension between individuality and corporateness. In church terms it is a continuation of the old striving for congregational control over against presbyterial or episcopal control—or vice-versa.

Comments on American Congregationalism

Vergilius Ferm's *Encyclopedia of Religion* (p. 196) provides a four phase outline of the phenomenon called Congregationalism. In brief it consists of,

1. reaction of certain Anglican clergy to the crown and consequent establishment of independent churches in the colonies,

2. a struggle between those with a Presbyterian bias and those holding a more democratic form of church government,

3. the solidification of Congregationalism in America,

4. growing awareness of the limitations of congregational polity and moves toward a more unified control.

The Congregational Church as an American denomination is not the object of our concern—congregational polity and spirit is. Presented in its best light American congregationalism is a movement which embodies a double principle: it advocates self-governance in local congregations and it confirms the right of alliance with congregations holding similar convictions and styles of life. But its point of great vulnerability is a matter of record—experiencing such lack of control and direction that it had to move self-consciously toward a national organization—its preoccupation with local autonomy dwarfed church-wide efforts. Individualistic polity insensitive to general corporate reality proved to be congregationalisms Achilles heel.

When our immigrant forefathers moved away from European influences and types of church government they did not enter a polity void. They orbited into the gravitational field of American congregationalism. The spirit of independence which infused it was most appealing. It appeared to complement the kind of congregational autonomy which was being attributed to Luther. And it certainly left its mark on American Lutheran church life. We have both benefited from its magnificent strengths and suffered from its monumental weaknesses.

Polity Developments within Lutheranism

We cannot trace our present ecclesiastical forms back to a pure congregational, or presbyterial, or episcopal polity. Absolute authority has never been posited in the congregation, or in a presbytery (a group of ruling elders), or in an episcopate (a monarchical priestly hierarchy). Before we try to describe what we have let's return to the Reformation era and catch some influences flowing out of that maelstrom which pre-date colonial Congregationalism by a century.

Luther's own circumstance is worth recalling. He rebelled against a church system which was the epitome of monarchical rule. Fulminations against popes and councils are unmistakable signs of his opposition to ecclesiastical autocracy. These have led some to conclude that Luther is one of the main sources of religious individualism and anarchy. But does the charge hold up? Can he be labeled "sire" of such movements? Roland Bainton, in *Here I Stand,* says definitely not!

Luther's individualism . . . is not the individualism of the Renaissance, seeking the fulfillment of the individual's capacities; it is not the individualism of the late scholastics, who on metaphysical grounds declared that reality consists only of individuals, and that aggregates like Church and state are not entities but simply the sum of their components. Luther was not concerned to philosophize about the structure of Church and state; his insistence was simply that every man must answer for himself to God. That was the extent of his individualism" (p. 141).

Luther's ambivalence regarding church polity simply presages our own. His paradoxes have become our paradoxes. While there is no direct polity line from him to us, the classic elements predominate. In one sense he was congregationalist, in another presbyterian, and in a third he even retained vestiges of episcopacy. Bainton observes that Luther could be at once to a degree the father of the congregationalism of the Anabaptists and of the territorial church of the later Lutherans" (p. 140f.).

Polity was not inconsequential for Luther but it was subordinate to something more important. Ecclesiology, the doctrine of the church, was what was really at stake. In replying to a Dominican who had been appointed to refute him, the

Reformer said, "You say that the Church consists representatively in the cardinals and virtually in the pope. I say that the Church consists virtually in Christ and representatively in a council. . . ." (Bainton, *The Reformation of the Sixteenth Century*, p. 41.) For him the ". . . Christian Church . . . is nothing else than the congregation, or assembly of the saints, i.e., the pious believing men on earth, which is gathered, preserved, and ruled by the Holy Ghost, and daily increased by means of the sacraments and the Word of God." (Hugh T. Kerr, *A Compend of Luther's Theology*, p. 123.) He understands *congregation* in two ways: it is particular in terms of the local congregation; it is universal in terms of being the whole Christian Church on earth.

As we move from Luther to post-Luther developments we should keep two things in mind—even though he described the church as "the communion of saints, . . . pious believing men on earth," he never thought of it in an exclusivistic Anabaptist way. Secondly, while it would be an error to equate the congregational emphases of Luther with congregationalist emphases which characterized colonial America, it should be pointed out that present Lutheranism has been influenced by both.

The Encyclopedia of the Lutheran Church has this to say about "The Structure of Lutheran Polity":

In setting up a new polity the reformers did not proceed from some ideal polity. . . . Nor did they single out any one particular polity as "divine." The reformers proceeded from the practical necessities of their day and the basic obligations of church life. . . . according to Lutheran thinking all matters of external church polity are subject to human insights and decisions; any polity is satisfactory as long as the two important marks are present and as long as it serves those two purposes.

The basic cell of the church is the local parish; . . . Most of the Lutheran "churches" understand themselves no longer as a union of more or less independent local congregations but, in accordance with Reformation principles, as a church united by a common confession and common responsibilities. (Vol. I, pp. 522-524. The ALC still uses the designation "union of congregations.")

Casual estimates of polity notwithstanding, Lutherans are very structure-conscious. We may have inherited an untidy polity arrangement, and it may seem that present polity has been put together by the same committee which, proverbially, started to design a horse and produced a camel, but we do have one. It is an amalgam of congregational and presbyterial elements, a mix of cellular and corporate components. It calls for living in structural, as well as theological, paradox. It resists absolutizing the congregational "cell" or the corporate denomination—though there are devotees of each. But at the heart of all Lutheran consciousness is a sterling conviction, something other than polity holds the church together. That something is a common confession of faith in Christ who is the real center of the church's life.

———

Since the Lutheran Church in America and the American Lutheran Church find considerable overlap in their life and work, definition of each is appropriate.

The Lutheran Church in America describes itself as "an inclusive fellowship and as local congregations gathered for worship and Christian Service" (Article IV The Nature of the Church). Sometimes it is popularly described as "congregations *and* ordained ministers." This language is taken from Article III (Membership), and ought not be lifted from its broader context and made the object of dichotomized review. When Henry Melchior Muhlenberg spearheaded the effort to gather immigrant Lutherans into congregations, he, in a sense, reprssented the church even when there were no congregations. Ergo the wording, "congregations and ordained ministers." In the Lutheran Church in America a pastor is a member of the congregation served and is also responsible to the total mission and discipline of the church.

In comparison, *The American Lutheran Church* describes itself as "a union of congregations . . ." (Constitution and Bylaws, Chapter 2. Purpose). This definition should be subject to the same contextual analysis used in dealing with the Lutheran Church in America documents. The former is an understanding which emerges out of a section on "The Nature of the Church." The latter is one portion of a statement which sets the context for the function of the congregation. While there appears to be a theoretical difference, both church bodies function in very similar ways in practice. Both are confessional. Both consider organization a negotiable item. Both are satisfied if the gospel and the sacraments are considered the priority items and marks of the church.

If the issue of dissimilarity is pressed let it be clear that the difference is not in the doctrine of the ministry or in the doctrine of the church. The contrast lies in the fact that in days past the Lutheran Church in America appears to have invested essential powers in the synods and residual powers in the national structure. Conversely The American Lutheran Church generally posits the essential powers in the national structure and residual powers in its districts. However, neither of these descriptions is absolute, modifications have taken place in both bodies.

Historically, each group comes from European antecedents. After the Peace of Augsburg in 1555, Lutherans and Roman Catholics emerged as the two officially recognized religious bodies in Germany. Lutherans became the dominant force in Scandinavia. In America it was different. Here Lutherans merited only minority classification. Professor Donald Huber, lecturing on the immigrant-minority status says:

> Immigrants are inclined to be tremendously insecure. Immigrant mentality begets social, religious, and economic conservatism. . . .

There is a reluctance to take risks. . . . Immigrants have made
. . . ethnicity the key to understanding their existence. In a way,
language, customs, and religion are frozen. . . . Such people find
it hard to cope with change and Lutherans are the least well
qualified to deal wtih this. . . . In terms of the church's life, the
polity question becomes a factor in the Lutheran identity crisis.
. . . Every time we talk merger there is "sweat over polity." This
is to say we use our polity as a security blanket.

What a dilemma! Theologically we claim "there is great
openness to polity change, there is no divine polity, all polity
matters are subject to human insight etc.," but psychologically
there is inordinate resistance to change and pathological defense of present forms. Thus we find a diffident stance on
the part of one denominational body over against other denominational bodies. Thus we find it all too commonplace to
have congregations posturing themselves over against their
own national bodies.

Such attitudes in congregations hurt the parent body; such
attitudes in denominational bureaucracies stunt the work of
basic units; such attitudes between church bodies make a
mockery of any claims to catholicity.

The Congregations—A Cellular Diagnosis

The biblical writers had an irresistable attraction to anatomical and biological metaphor. God is described humanly—
"his head and his hair were white as white wool, . . . his
eyes were like a flame of fire, . . . his voice was like the sound
of many waters, . . . his face was like the sun shining in full
strength. . . . His right hand and his holy arm have gotten him
the victory. . . . Who has known the mind of the Lord? . . ."
Humanness is the very vehicle of revelation, "The Word
became flesh and dwelt among us . . . he who has seen me
has seen the Father". This anthropomorphic language—de-
scribing God in human terms—is not only true for the "head",

it is true for the "body", the church. Anatomical analogies abound, "we are members together in the body of Christ," senses, organs, and extremities are used in graphic fashion.

These descriptions all predate the language and categories of modern science, yet Christian preachers and teachers in our context find it perfectly consistent to take the complexities of biological structure and life as we now know them, and again, analogically, portray the truth of God. A new dimension is discoverable through the microscope, but not a new truth. Thus conversation about "cells".

The encyclopedic description is that "the basic cell of the church is the local parish." Unless there is robust health intramurally within the cell as well as inter-cellularly throughout the structure, the corporate body is in peril. But just how important is each cell?

Right after the Second World War the great Japanese Christian, Toyohiko Kagawa spoke at the Methodist Temple in downtown Chicago. Here was a man born of a concubine mother who really didn't even know his father. Yet, through faith in Christ he had become one of the real moving forces in world Christianity. With less than perfect English he talked about "dying that the body might live". "If you cut your arm" he said, "the red blood corpuscles rush to the wound, expose themselves, and die! But in their dying a scab is formed and the body lives. If the blood cells do not do this life will perish". He was of course referring to the lives of individual Christians and congregations and citing their importance for the universal church.

Similarly, a fine medical internist had the question put to him, "how significant can one cell be among millions of cells in the body?" "Well" he replied, "you can measure its significance this way—each cell starts out as a rather rectangular block below the level of the skin. As it rises toward the epidermal surface it flattens out and finally flakes off. It is programmed to function in this way. If it doesn't, if for some reason it defies the genetic code, it becomes what we call a cancerous cell. And the worst part is that it reproduces others."

In personal and congregational terms this gives us real pause for reflection. Are we functioning according to the "sacrificial code" endemic to the body of Christ? Are we losing our lives for his sake so that we may find them? If not, why not? Perhaps that can be answered from two approaches to illness: first, from a pathology which begins in the cell; second, from a pathology in which the whole body is involved. Simply put, one cell can make the body sick, and sometimes the body can make each cell sick.

Let's examine this as a theological metaphor from both sides: a pathological condition in the body, i.e., the denomination, can jeopardize the life of otherwise healthy individual cells, congregations. This is a factor in our social malaise and limited effectiveness. There has been limited churchwide strategy in which local units were involved—and this translates as non-caring. Waste, apathy, and indecisive planning on national and district levels has profound effects on basic cell units. But those things have had their review in previous chapters. For this moment let us keep our focus directed toward the cell and its histolysis, diagnosing ills which arise within this basic unit.

Congregational polity, when utilized as a self-contained and locally directed polity, is a detrimental factor in the life of the church. Whatever positive support can be marshaled on behalf of Luther's congregationalism, Lutheran congregationalism, or general American congregationalism, the fact is that within our culture, congregationalism has become all too regularly a polity expression justifying private concerns. We have moved from the individualism of the person to the individualism of the congregation, but the movement has been essentially centripetal, turned inward! Congregational agendas and local concerns have become the sine qua non.

Normal expectations regarding the corporate concerns of the church go awanting. What can be said other than "a congregation whose ego lacks the 'code motivation of sacrifice' will seldom be a force for the healing of the nations"? Unless a congregation concedes that when it becomes a member cell in a church body it gives up part of its freedom and life for greater purpose and life, it can only live in truncated congregationalism—distorted polity.

A second type of illness arises out of self-pity and a sense of exploitation. There are times, right or wrong, when parish people say "we feel used". The dulcet tones of national and district leaders sound the call for monetary contributions, the long arm of the denomination is there to collect them. Some feel it's all a one way street. "Everything goes from us to them!" Hyperbole? Most certainly. But not totally devoid of truth. Yet, self-pity can become a consuming process in which self-excusing is never apprised, and real potential is never evaluated. How then are the cells to know how well they are really doing? Yet, hyperbolic complaint gets to be accepted as reasoned estimate. Are congregations used? Absolutely. That is part of their cellular reason for being, but this doesn't diminish the need for care and attention from the parent body.

But perhaps the most critical point of vulnerability is in the nucleus, viz., in leadership personality. Pastors' personalities have a great deal to do with congregation's personalities. If they are sour, or if they have some kind of vendetta against the denomination, they will hurt the denomination all right, but they will also hurt the congregation and themselves. Performance seldom rises above personal capacity to sacrifice —but, these liabilities and weaknesses notwithstanding, sickness is not what I wish to emphasize.

Years ago I purchased an edition of Cecil's Textbook of Medicine. It was overwhelming. Count the number of diseases you know and multiply them by a thousand. You'll still not cover the ills that plague mankind. I read that tome with increasing despair—"My God, the afflictions flesh is heir to!" One of my friends laughed at that and said, "you better quit reading Cecil and letting your imagination run away with you. If you really want something to think about, consider the constancy of your own health in the face of all that disease." Great advice, and how it does apply to the church. The amazing thing is not all that is wrong, or can go wrong, or that is immediately threatening, the amazing thing is that the church is as healthy as it is.

The "body" is constantly beleaguered by enemies from without and by infidelity from within. Alien philosophies are an incessant challenge—secularism and atheism are destructive cancerous agents. Internally there is compromise and self-seeking and smallness of heart. But the astonishing fact stands, American Lutheranism has an essential well-being.

The Denomination—A Regimen for Corporate Health

Like persons, we've abused the body and developed some bad habits. None of those things should be concealed. We have also done some things right, and these should be commended. What is needed is a conscious effort to promote and preserve health and the church should be every bit as intentional about that as the diligent but over-weight, out of condition, business man who goes to see his physician.

The regimen must emerge from the national office and district office—these are only popular designations for leaders, polity, and mandated areas of work. This leadership has no greater responsibility than care of the body and care of the cells. But how do they affect it? By autocratic means and monarchical control? Not at all. They do it by example and word. They pursue those things necessary for the health of any body. Let us elaborate on each:

1. *A body must take proper nourishment*—for Christians this means subsisting on the Word (of which the sacraments are an expression). The church lives "by every word that proceeds from the mouth of God." It cannot exude health if it feeds on human words and philosophies. For young Christians, milk is the proper diet but for mature Christians, solid food. This means going beyond "the first principles of God's Word" and sharing those things which are more difficult and complex.

2. *A body must digest that which is eaten*—but just how do we do that? I think by the use of our critical capacities. The ability to reason should be for the life of the mind and spirit what digestive capacities are for the body. If liver, pancreas and bile are not working we will most surely grow ill. It is time for us to state the other side of the adage "reason is the devil's whore." "Reason can also be the handmaid of the Lord." We must be able to study, critically reflect on, and absorb the truth of God.

3. *Every healthy body must exercise*—this too has implications for the church. Faith active in love is how the church exercises. It is obvious that we are not in the best of condition. We've loved the lovable, rejected the unlovable, and politely ignored many of the unloved. Our eating habits are better than our exercising habits and we can profit mightily by letting this be a new part, or a more expansive part, of our regimen.

4. *Health also demands the elimination of waste*—a body which cannot eliminate waste is in peril. Uremic poisoning is deadly. And so is the perpetuation of things in a church system which are condoned and protracted when they should have been eliminated. Examples: Racism built on a spurious interpretation of some Bible passages; chauvinism, be it male or female; parochialism, especially the hyper-Lutheran kind; priestly superiority; and an irresponsible sanctioning of culture.

5. *A healthy body also reproduces*—without reproduction everything is in jeopardy. If healthy cells do not reproduce the prognosis for the body is bad. Cells must reproduce to take the place of older cells which may have completed their function. They must help the body to grow. They must be faithful to their code information. And if our corporate body, the denomination, is not reproducing it is not carrying out its

role in the family of God. Evangelism by word and deed is what we are dealing with.

The fact that the church is expressing willingness to exercise sacrificial power is reason for cautious optimism. Cells once obsessed with self-serving concerns are turning outward —so too is the body. It's all quite biblical and very exciting.

The Combination "Par Excellence"

The purpose of this analog odyssey is to surface with a constructive view of the church in its local expression and also of the church in its denominational role. It is all too easy to bad-mouth either or both. But it would be a tragedy to let the accent remain on tensions which exist between cells and corporate body with no effort to understand them in a constructive, though paradoxical, sense. The truth is that one cannot exist without the other, and therefore both are involved in an interdependency which is critical. The denomination must care for its congregations. Only thus will it allay suspicions of neglect and avert ultimate hostility. Congregations must care for the parent body. Only thus can the church effectively address the needs of the world, only thus can the indictment be stayed, "you are just building your own little kingdom."

It seems to me that the ideal is to have congregations with a *collective mind* and a denomination with a *corrective spirit.* That is, congregations must transcend local self-interest and learn to posture themselves in relation to the corporate body. The denomination, concommittantly, is corrective in a self-correcting way. This does not mean acting like big brother with an inquisitorial attitude and correcting congregations. It means being accountable for the leadership, and work, and resources trusted to national and district offices.

There is no shorter cut to credibility.

7 THE AMERICAN LUTHERAN CHURCH AND THE CHURCH CATHOLIC

It is good for us Lutherans, as it is for all Christians, to see ourselves as others see us. Viewing our corporate self through the eyes of others is, however, a formidable task. The problem has less to do with the number of observers than it has to do with the discomfort of receiving adverse opinions. We covet approbation and make that the expectation, but when those beyond our circle of intimacy criticize, and evidence little effort to affirm us, we find their comments hard to take. The degree of difficulty notwithstanding, we must be sensitive seers and hearers lest our self estimates prove illusory and lead us into mental ghettos.

An illustrative case of critiquing is to be found in this disarming evaluation of German Lutherans from Eberhard Busche's biography of Karl Barth:

In December Barth repeated his serious hesitations about the German Lutherans in a letter to the American Sylvester Michelfelder. . . . He expressed his suspicions of their "persistent confessional romanticism, their stubborn association with political reaction, their obscure ritual romanticizing, their feeble attitude at the time of the church struggle and more recently their sabotage of the unity of the Evangelical Church of Germany by splitting and forming the National Evangelical Lutheran Church of Germany." (*Karl Barth,* p. 366.)

"Those were German Lutherans" we protest, "let the indictment rest with them!" But honesty will not permit it.

There is too much truth about all Lutherans in Barth's verdict. We all share in those failings. Even if certain of his allegations can be refuted or modified in their application to American Lutherans, his statement must be taken with consumate seriousness. Our ability to weigh its charges and accept its judgments with grace will prove the measure of our integrity and our maturity.

The Constructive Acceptance of Criticism

What makes it possible for any individual or institution to use criticism constructively? How can some accept the withering accusations of others and incorporate them in their own process of self-examination? If we discover persons or groups with such incorporative abilities, we can be sure of one thing —certain preconditions are in effect. These include admission of fallibility, recognition that truth is greater than our awareness of it, and, most of all, grace. With sin affecting the totality of being, mind as well as heart, grace is as much corrective for our mental inflexibility as it is for our moral infidelity.

What critiques, or who criticizes, is important. We must know where authentic appraisals emanate from before we can focus them as criticisms of the self by the self. Five such sources are preeminent. Frequently they overlap, and there are even times when they seem to be identical. Here is the order:

1. The Word of God which is both the constitutive and the judging reality for the church.
2. Members from the other major Lutheran church bodies.
3. Christians in other households of faith.
4. The society around us.
5. That small, but persistent, voice of conscience.

The Word is the incarnate Word to whom the words of Scripture testify. He addresses us through the holy writings not simply as "a God who has spoken" but as "the Christ who is speaking." The Word brings the church into being. He comes from God, he animates and directs. The church must therefore seek to live *coram deo,* that is, in the presence of God. This Word which constitutes also judges. The church cannot prosper unless the Word is allowed to fulfil both constituting and judging functions. Left to its own devising the church will inevitably distort, and deny, and subvert. But God is adamant that the church live by his Word and not men's words—therefore the church is always in the process of being reformed, reshaped. This is what is meant by the Protestant principle and what theologians mean by *semper reformanda,* always being reformed.

Lutherans are also under frequent review by those in sister churches. Sometimes their dispassionate critique hardens into passionate criticism and we recoil at it. "Objectively" it may even be unwarranted or wrong, but we can never evade the necessity of listening. Necessity? Who establishes that? Among others, all Lutherans since the Reformation. Our very forebears set a premium on listening and evaluating. They tested all spirits by God's Word and reason, and they bequeathed us a most functional paradox: on one side they advocated "the right of private interpretation," on the other they insisted that interpretation and life were subject to the winess and the confessions of the church throughout all ages.

Within this last decade a large segment of the Lutheran family risked being reviewed by brothers and sisters from the far reaches of the globe. In a *Report of the Mission on Six Continents Consultation,* some pungent, but not unloving, observations came forth:

—Congregations are merely a mirror of their community, socially and economically. Can the congregation raise a prophetic voice? (p. 30)

—The church is called to devise a strategy in its ministry which attacks injustice in the structures of society. (p. 33)

—culture and heritage play a more important role than theology. (p. 34)

—All your social assistance is understood in individual terms. . . . that implies not wanting to judge the social structure of your system. . . . (p. 36)

—I have felt clearly the *scandal* of your denominationalism. (p. 38)

—Many pastors and lay persons use the differences in historical background as an excuse. The past is thus kept artificially alive. . . . (p. 40)

Subjecting our corporate life, convictions, and practice to peers proved to be penetratingly painful. We like to believe that we are better for having done it. Lutherans, admittedly, are only a part of the church catholic. Most of us concede that our life and doctrine should not be restricted to Reformation categories and sister church review. We willingly enter the ecumenical arena, not to relativize the truth we believe but, to witness to the relevance of him who is Truth and who stands over the whole church. Old ways of relating to other traditions are no longer adequate, nor are old ways of formulating problems adequate. Out of the broader context new voices speak to us, new challenges are raised for us:

Does anyone still ask with Luther: "How does God's rule come about in man?" Or with the Council of Trent: "How does sinful man reach a state of grace?" Apart from theologians, who regard all old questions as eternal questions, who is there to argue about these things?
If we set out schematically the old and the new statement of the problem, it looks like this:
Formerly the question was asked in great cosmic and spiritual anguish: how do I get a gracious God?
But now the question is asked with no less cosmic and existential anguish: how does my life acquire a meaning?
Formerly this God was seen as God the judge who acquits man from his sin and declares him just.

Now he is seen as God the partner who calls man to freedom and to responsibility for world and history.
Formerly it was a question of individual justification and of "saving our souls" in a purely personal sense.
Now it is a question of the social dimension of salvation and of all-round care of our fellow men.
Formerly people were concerned in a spiritual sense with salvation hereafter and peace with God.
Now they are concerned wholly and entirely with social conditions and the reform or even revolution of structures.
Formerly man was constrained to justify his life before God.
Now he is constrained to justify his life to himself and his fellow men. (Hans Küng, *On Being a Christian*, pp. 581-582.

It is not just other Lutherans and other Christians like Hans Küng, however, who call us to account. Even the secular society represented in the Terkel interviews challenges the church. What terrible irony inheres in the statement, "I was away from the church for two years, and I learned more about myself and my problems and the world than in thirty-five years of going to confession." And if all of this weren't enough, there is still that haunting thing called conscience, the voice in the heart which none of us can escape. Others may scoff at it and demean it, but for the Christian community Barth was right when he said "Conscience is the perfect interpreter of life."

As postulated, it takes the humility of a confessed fallibiilty, the acknowledgment of God's ultimate truth, and an awful lot of grace to cope with criticism from others as well as with one's own self-criticism. A church which can accept criticism will not only be chastened, but blessed. A church which cannot will inevitably cant toward sectarianism and will make its scandal of an outdated, unloving, and bigoted expression of Christianity, a substitute for the real *skandalon*—the cross of our Lord Jesus Christ. It was out of this concern that these words were forged to become a part of our inter-church record:

Criticism from without will always have some effect. It may reinforce prejudices already in control or it can generate honest review which eventuates in change. But the desired condition is that critical self-analysis emerge from within. To have that, a church must not only believe in the Reformation, but carry through the continuing reformation of the body of Christ. Without this, churches become sects. . . . (*Toward Understanding One Another*, LCMS/ALC Commission on Fellowship, Feb. 29, 1980, p. 5.)

When a denomination is viewed in relationship to the wider world and the great church catholic, there is a tendency for some to stay in the microcosm. "World" and "church catholic" constitute a threat. "We do not want our values compromised by a sick naturalism—we do not want our truth equivocated by the uncommitted in interchurch dialogs." Sad? Yes, but the insulated life that people construct in closed groups is deemed preferable to the exposure, and possible benefits, which might be experienced in the macrocosm. Nostalgically they fantasize the past, the importance of persons and events, the values they say were in operation, the constancy of life. Thus commences the process of re-tribalization, searching for meaning and purpose in one's roots and clan, one's homeland, one's culture, one's religious tradition. Churches in this syndrome will not easily die, but neither will they have a significant effect on the life of the world. These are the types Barth labels "social reactionaries."

The Church Catholic's Contribution to New Vision

The Wisdom writer's words are not only immortal, they are instructive. "Where there is no vision the people perish" (Prov. 29:18). He could only utter this as a caring person and one who knew the obverse, "where there is vision the people live!" All kinds of aggrieved human circumstances and mortal

116

ills can be endured, if there is vision. But who defines vision, and how? Strange people claim strange things. What are we to believe? The church catholic has held to a consistent testimony throughout all ages. "The biblical vision is the only trustworthy vision for both man and world!" God's intent is clearly imaged in the New Jerusalem, the holy city of God. This is the vision by which all penultimate visions and penultimate claims are to be judged. It moves from the future back to the present.

Lutherans must orient themselves anew to this way of thinking. I say anew because the vision is part of the church's life; it is latently there even though it has been subsumed under other concerns. Our natural tendency is to take our cues from the past, seeking inspiration and direction from what has been. But the past is not our future and it isn't our present. However, let no one deduce from this that history should be disdained. History may only be today's reflection on what happened yesterday, but there are times when the future invades the present in a way that alters reality and influences coming events. Then history is not only a record of the past, it is a prolog to what is yet to be. This is the great contradiction—we must appeal to history in order to transcend history.

The early church fathers help us to do that. Consider the work of Hermas, The Shepherd; Irenaeus, and his concept of recapitulation, and Augustine, with the City of God. "The Shepherd," as it is popularly called, contains a series of visions intending to call the church to repentance and to redirect its life. The author considered Christians the third race besides the Romans and the Jews. He was not rehearsing genetics. Over against traditional ethnic distinctions, he was an advocate for a people who defied description. An enigma to others, they had taken their cue from the future and how that future did inform their present! Jesus Christ was that future's word. He himself was the sign of a new unity, but more than a sign. He was the very occasion of that unity.

117

A striking illustration of the significance of the new people is given in *The Shepherd of Hermas,* a book written at the beginning of the second century. The writer sees some mountains of different appearance and colour and asks the Shepherd what this signifies. The Shepherd explains that these mountains represent people who differ in opinion and disposition. The writer then sees stones being taken from these hills to build a tower and notices that the stones are scarcely put in position before they take all the same colour and acquire the same shining whiteness. The Shepherd explains that the stones are men drawn from very different peoples who "are united in the same faith and the same love. . . . the stones become all of the same whiteness—for belonging to the people of Christ, the life in Christ, creates an indestructible bond, and brings to birth a community united from above which is stronger than all the communities united from below.

These first Christians did not only dream of this new people. They *were* that people.

Hermas' vision was drawn from the New Testament vision— it depicted God's kingdom, future and present, and the Lamb who brought people into a new relationship. As hearers grasped that vision and allowed it to inform their lives, they had evidence that what was to be, was.

Irenaeus, along with Origen and Clement of Alexandria, held Hermas in high esteem. His concept of recapitulation was meant to have a similar impact. Irenaeus built his theology on the realities of Adam's disobedience and Christ's redeeming life. He saw the old aeon under Adam dominated by sin and death. The world lies under condemnation. However, a new thing has happened. The future, replete with life, is brought into the present by Jesus Christ. With Paul, Irenaeus proclaims Christ as the new Adam. He reinstitutes the process of growth interrupted and imperiled by the first Adam's sin.

When He became incarnate, Christ "recapitulated in Himself the long sequence of mankind," and passed through all the stages of human life, sanctifying each in turn. As a result (and this is Irenaeus's main point), just as Adam was the originator of a race disobedient and doomed to death, so Christ can be regarded as inaugurating a new, redeemed humanity. (J.N.D. Kelly, *Early Christian Doctrine*, p. 173.)

Justo L. Gonzalez also sees Christ as the center of Irenaeus' theology:

In Christ, that image according to which and for which man was made has come to dwell among men. This is the work . . . which Irenaeus calls "recapitulation." . . . Christ's recapitulation is a new starting point; . . . the history of the old Adam is repeated, although in an opposite direction . . . this . . . continues until the final consummation. . . . The church has an important role in this work of recapitulation. . . . in Christ the whole church overcomes Satan because Christ is the head of the Church. (*A History of Christian Thought*, Vol. 1, pp. 169-171.)

Christ appears in history and is a part of history; he is in the old aeon but he brings the new aeon. He redeems those who have lived in the past, he is the Word of Life for today, and he is the promise of a future in God. For Christians, that future is experienced in the now.

The classic and most enduring of the works of the fathers is St. Augustine's *The City of God*. It speaks for itself:

We give the name of the city of God unto that society whereof that Scripture bears witness, which has gained the most exalted authority and preeminence over all other works whatsoever, by the disposing of the divine providence, not the chance decisions of men's judgments. For there it is said: "Glorious things are spoken of thee, thou city of God": and in another place: "Great is the Lord, and greatly to be praised in the city of our God, even upon His holy mountain, increasing the joy of all the earth." . . . These testimonies, and thousands more, teach us that there is a city of God, whereof His inspired love makes us desire to be members. The earthly citizens prefer their gods before this heavenly city's holy Founder, knowing not that He is the God of gods, . . . (Vol. 1, p. 312)

The contemporary futurists have a penultimate word for us, and one which we should heed. But it is St. John, writer of the Apocalypse, and Hermas, and Irenaeus, and Augustine who point us to the ultimate one. The diminished sense of eschatology and the lack of attention given to the Eternal City in our church's life has an amazing congruency with its ineffectiveness. Confessional romanticism cannot compensate for lost eschatological vision. The gravitational pull of the future must overcome the inertial drag of the past.

What does our church need? What does it need to be? An inexorable consensus is emerging in response to those questions. Our people want a church that is biblically faithful, future oriented, socially conscious, and ecumenically daring! All of this comes to a head in the most crucial ecclesiological issue before us, unity in Christ and Lutheran unification. Each of the partners contemplating that unification embodies virtues and vices, great strengths and glaring weaknesses. What Lutherans corporately decide may be assuredly within the will of God, or quite contrary to it, but no one should decide anything without the consciousness that the church is Christ's, not ours, and his will is that his church be one.

Unity in Christ and Lutheran Unification

It is axiomatic that God has created the unity of the church in and through Jesus Christ and that we either witness to it or detract from it. All Christians must start with this as a "given." We are admonished that "the unity of the church is not something to be achieved by Christians." It is a gift ". . . given in Christ and through Christ." Just as every gift implies a faithful response so this gift of unity, already ours, suggests movement toward unification. In the Lutheran World Federation document *Christ Frees and Unites* the authors, having acknowledged unity as a gift, lay great stress on unity as an obligation of the church:

The unity which the Church has in Christ is a hidden reality only to be apprehended by faith. But this unity is not something that can remain "invisible"; it must be manifested. For this reason the members of the Church have a holy obligation and a great responsibility. Certainly the unity of the Church is not one which we as Christians can create. But we are responsible nevertheless to see that this unity be given its proper expression.

In all our attempts to manifest the unity of the Church we must bear in mind what the true nature of the Church is, and be guided by it. We dare not desire a man-made "unity at any price" but only that unity which Christ has given his Church by means of his act of redemption. Those who know themselves to be united in faith should express their oneness and fellowship (pp. 14-15).

In a technical sense, therefore, Lutherans ought not to talk about their unity or general Christian unity suggesting that essential unity is contingent on the efforts of church leaders or followers. What we should talk about and do something about is our disunited state and how we can manifest God's unity in the unification of Lutherans. This all sounds like double-talk and may be largely a matter of semantics, but we pursue a two-fold apologetic which advances unity as a divine gift and unification as an obligatory human response.

What about diversity within unity? Twenty years ago the stress was on unity, or more properly, unification. Today the stress appears to be on diversity. Some who favor this category take their rationale from Paul's discourse in 1 Corinthians 12, equating the parts of the body with various denominations. That isn't how the Apostle exegetes his metaphor. He parallels bodily part with the representative labors of apostles, prophets, teachers, workers of miracles, etc. These are functional offices within the body and constitute diversity of function. They are not church segments indicating divisiveness of form. It is not proper to take passages dealing with the diversity of functions, or offices, and exegete them so as to justify denominational separatedness.

The cause of Christ is not helped when those wanting to emphasize unity-unification ignore legitimate questions of diversity. We are cautioned to ". . . bear in mind what the true nature of the Church is, and be guided by it. We dare not desire a man-made 'unity at any price' . . ." But neither is Christ's cause helped when others take the factor of diversity and transpose it into disunity. Then even a benign thesis like reconciled diversity can be used to baptize a divided state, the logic being if Christ has reconciled us in our diversity there is no great compulsion to achieve outward oneness. We, ". . . members of the Church have a holy obligation and a great responsibility . . . to see that this unity be given its proper expression." (Ibid. p. 15).

How should Lutherans view the current scene? Historically they begin by pointing to the fact that Lutheranism is not indigenous to our country. As a European export two main factors influenced its American development, old world nationalism and culture, and, the struggle between American theology and European confessionalism. Small groups, or synods, banded together and became churches. At the turn of the century there were 54 identifiable Lutheran groups on this continent. The atomized state of Lutheranism pointed these church bodies toward unification, and some dramatic changes occurred. Lutheran euphoria with new configurations, however, might well be tempered with a comment from Niebuhr's notebook,

What we accomplish in the way of church unity ought to be accepted with humility and not hailed with pride. We are not creating. We are merely catching up with creation. (Op. cit. p. 90.)

The question for some is Have we gone too far?; for others, Have we arrived?; and for still others, Have we gone far enough? From my perspective, the only legitimate question is the last one. But if there is disquiet about limited progress, it can only be dealt with by an honest probe of those things which impede progress. So we ask the question—"Does Dr. E. Clifford Nelson's observation regarding impediments faced between 1914-1970 hold?"

Lutheran unity efforts in the 20th century . . . usually foundered on three or four major problems: the relation of the Word of God to the Scriptures, and confessions . . . 'unionism', 'ecumenism', and membership of pastors in lodges. (*Lutheranism in America 1914-1970*, p. 183.)

No, these are not the issues of this hour. Vis-a-vis those cited by the eminent historian as critical for the first six decades of this century, the challenging factors now appear to be personalities, polity, ecclesiastical power, parish involvement, and procrastination.

I do not wish to be acerbic in suggesting that personalities are something of a critical factor. They have always been a factor. We are dealing with essentially good people, but each of these good persons has a lot of self invested in the church as it is. . . . Polity is a big iceberg and one on which unification efforts could be dashed, yet even the largest of floes melts.

We must never allow polity to be our master—it is our servant! If we agree with others on the true nature of the church, and know ourselves to be united in faith, we should unflinchingly stick to the intention of unification and make polity serve Christ's church and the world's needs. . . . Power, and every human's thirst for it, comes to us in innocent guise. Why deceive ourselves and act as though it isn't a reality? . . . Parish involvement signifies a growing grass roots demand for participation in decisions affecting local units that will have to be honored as never before. . . . And then, procrastination; this is the most seductive element and in a way the biggest hurdle of all. It enervates every good impulse—"We're not quite sure . . . things may be better later . . . no one has given us a clear mandate." So "the native air of resolution is sicklied o'er with the pale cast of thought; And enterprises of great pith and moment . . . their currents turn away, And lose the name of action." (Shakespeare, *Hamlet.*)

Leadership in this hour can distinguish itself only if it shows that it can cope with the factors of personality, polity, power, parish involvement, and procrastination. Mergers, consolidations, unifications can be built only on purpose and principle centered in Christ's unity. The rest is sand.

Lest possibilities are lost in the fog of unanswered questions, let's try to clear the atmosphere:

In pressing for unification, isn't the consequent re-structuring a waste of time, energy, and resources?

No. As Reinhold Niebuhr said, "We . . . need a constant reorganization of social processes and systems, so that society will not aggravate but mitigate the native imperialistic impulses of man." Sensitive souls may be shocked by paralleling other social organizations and churches when dealing with "the imperialistic impulses of man" but they are there even in the church.

There are more positive reasons, however, for exposing oneself and one's church to the rigors of unification, and they have to do with momentum and effectiveness. Without change or challenge every operation moves closer to inertia and ineffectiveness. What major industry does not continuously challenge its way of doing things, its leadership, its alignment with competitors and subsidiaries?

The positive reasons for pursuing unification in the church far outweigh the negative "curbing of the imperialistic impulses in man", however needed, and such expenditure does not represent waste.

Isn't cooperation without unification a better alternative?

No. Cooperation devours more energy and time and resources than consolidation. Moreover, it never effects as much. Invariably cooperation gets shunted to the project level where it gets due praise, but never poses a threat to disguised aggression and competitive purpose. Cooperation means the retention of double, or treble systems, when one would do.

Wouldn't it be better to work for Christian unification instead of Lutheran unification?

This should not be an either/or question nor should it have an either/or answer. Lutheran unification is but a projected step in what is now perceived as a very long process of Christian unification. It sounds heroic to say "let's not work on Lutheran relationships when we could be working on more expansive ones, like those with the Reformed or the Roman Catholics." But this rhetoric lacks realism.

It is proper that we should first deal most intimately, honorably, and collegially with our closest spiritual kin, the Lutherans. If we cannot accomplish anything with them, or with a part of them, how can we expect to do more with others? Old antipathies have faded, for which we all thank God, but it was a Dominican priest, heavily involved in a theological consortium and in ecumenical concerns who said "Rome doesn't want to deal with the Lutherans piece-meal." We must get ourselves together first.

Isn't unification finally, and only, an intra-mural issue for the church?

Small yes, big no. Of course its immediate effect will be in the lives of the church bodies involved, but finally the unity of the church in Christ, and the unification of Lutherans, and the re-unification of all Christians is not just for the sake of the church. It is, as Gerhard Forde says, for the sake of the world!

When the church is united in faith, the world sees a common witness to Christ; when it is united in form, it interfaces the world with an institutional solidarity; when it is united in function, the world receives the fruits of its ministry which are single-minded proclamation and single-hearted diaconal service.

Lastly, is there a feasible stance to be taken?

More than we know, more than many care to know. How feasible was it for the 16th century Reformers to go the second, or the third mile? They endured the calumny of Rome and saw Luther excommunicated. The only feasible stance seemed to be a defensive one with survival as the aim. In spite of all the discordant things in that moment of history, they came to the Diet of Augsburg and appeared before the emperor in a most remarkable spirit and with an extra-ordinary intent. It is strikingly clear in their Preface to the Augsburg Confession:

In connection with the matter pertaining to the faith and in conformity with the imperial summons, . . .

we offer and present a confession of our pastors' and preachers' teaching and of our own faith, setting forth how and in what manner, on the basis of the Holy Scriptures, these things are preached, taught, communicated, and embraced in our lands, principalities, dominions, cities, and territories. . . .

If the other electors, princes, and estates also submit a similar written statement of their judgments and opinions, in Latin and German, we are prepared, in obedience to Your Imperial Majesty, our most gracious lord, to discuss with them and their associates, in so far as this can honorably be done, such practical and equitable ways as may restore unity. Thus the matters at issue between us may be presented in writing on both sides, they may be discussed amicably and charitably, our differences may be reconciled, and we may be united in one, true religion, even as we are all under one Christ and should confess and contend for Christ. . . .

If, however, our lords, friends, and associates who represent the electors, princes, and estates of the other party do not comply with the procedure intended by Your Imperial Majesty's summons, if no amicable and charitable negotiations take place between us, and if no results are attained, nevertheless we on our part shall not omit doing anything, in so far as God and conscience allow, that may serve the cause of Christian unity. (Tappert ed. pp. 25-26.)

Nevertheless we on our part shall not omit doing anything . . . that may serve the cause of Christian unity. If those at Augsburg were magnanimous enough to view papal relationships with this kind of charity, why should any modest moves toward Lutheran unification be eroded by doubts of feasibility?

Frightful threats hang over the human community, atomic weapons for warfare, atomic leaks in peace. The Frankenstein aspects of genetic manipulation are only starting to dawn on us. Fuel supplies dwindle, there is an imbalance in edible goods, and a monetary system is blowing up in our faces. We chafe at an upsurge of militant philosophies and a burgeoning secularism which seems irresistible. Despair seems to be the only logical alternative.

It is crucial, therefore, that the church hear again the undaunted words of that visionary Paul:

. . . the transcendent power belongs to God and not to us. We are afflicted in every way, but not crushed; perplexed, but not driven to despair; persecuted, but not forsaken; struck down, but not destroyed, always carrying in the body the death of Jesus, so that the life of Jesus may also be manifested in our bodies (2 Cor. 4:7-10).

So Lutheran Christians face the future with anticipation, not immobilized by anxiety and quite ready to do battle with despair. We know the transitory nature of things. Death is death for us, too, whether it comes by an aborigine's stone hatchet, the plague, being run over by a Model T, or perishing in an atomic blast. But as members of the "third race" we affirm the Apostle's witness and identify with all those who

. . . died . . . not having received what was promised, but having seen it and greeted it from afar, and having acknowledged that they were strangers and exiles on the earth. . . . But as it is, they desire a better country, that is, a heavenly one. Therefore God is not ashamed to be called their God, for he has prepared for them a city (Heb. 11:13-16).

That is what lies ahead and what God beckons us to. That is also the coming reality God gives to inform and correct this human present, and blessed are those who are in league with his future.